THE DIVINE WEAVER

By Joan Beacock

The following story is one woman's fight from innocence to reality, and of finding a reason in life through faith in Jesus Christ.

Show me thy ways, O Lord, teach me thy paths.
Psalm c25.v4

warcrypress.co.uk
Joan Beacock (c)

ISBN: 9781912543069

THE DIVINE WEAVER - Produced by wacrypress.co.uk (part of Roobix Ltd: 7491233) on behalf of Joan Beacock Copyright © Joan Beacock 2018.

Joan Beacock has asserted his right as the author of this work in accordance with the Copyright, Designs and Patents Act 1988.

Original jacket illustration by various historical / religious images

Printed and bound in Great Britain by Clays, St. Ives

This book is dedicated to:-

Pastor Grossmith. We thank God for him
and the gift He gave him.

Life is but a weaving
Quoted by Corrie ten Boom

My life is but a weaving
Between my God and me.
I cannot choose the colours
He weaveth steadily.

Oft times he weaveth sorry;
And I in foolish pride
Forget he sees the upper
And I the underside

Not til the loom is silent
And the shuttles cease to fly
Will God unroll the canvas
And reveal the reason why.

The dark threads are as needful
In the weavers skilful hand
As the threads of gold and silver
In the pattern he has planned.

He knows, He loves, He cares
Nothing this truth can dim
He gives the very best to those
Who leave the choice to him.

Job c13.

14 Why do I put myself in jeopardy and take
my life in my hands?

15 Though he slay me, yet will I hope in him.

16 Indeed, this will turn out for my deliverance,
for no godless man would dare come before
him!

Malachi c3.

16 Then those who feared the Lord talked with each
other, and the Lord listened and heard. A scroll of
remembrance was written his presence concerning
those who feared the Lord and honoured his name.

17 "They will be mine," says the Lord Almighty, in the
day when I make up my treasured possession. I will
spare them, just as in compassion a man spares his son
who serves him.

18 And you will again see the distinction between the
righteous and the wicked, between those who serve God
and those who do not.

Deuteronomy c18.

9 When you enter the land the Lord your God is giving
you, do not learn to imitate the detestable ways of the
nations there.

10 Let no-one be found among you who sacrifices his
son or daughter in the fire, who practices divination or
sorcery, interprets omens, engages in witchcraft,

11 or casts spells, or is a medium or spiritist or who consults the dead.

12 Anyone who does these things is detestable to the Lord, and because of these detestable practices the Lord you God will drive out those nations before you.

13 You must be blameless before the Lord your God.

Matthew c12

28 But if I drive out demons by the spirit of God, then the kingdom of God has come upon you.

29 Or again, how can anyone enter a strong man's house and carry off his possessions unless he first ties up the strong man? Then he can rob his house.

Acknowledgements

For all the help given, all the friendship and the hours of counselling, my thanks go to Andrew McRae.

To my husband George for helping me put the manuscript together.

I thank God for Gail Hunter and all her hard work in sorting out this book from start to finish.

My thanks also go to dear Gladys and Alan, for all their shared prayers over the years for our family.

Contents

Chapter 1   1

Chapter 2   20

Chapter 3   31

Chapter 4   46

Chapter 5   68

Chapter 6   85

Chapter 7   106

Chapter 8   118

Chapter 9   128

Chapter 10   141

Chapter 11   157

1

There's a friend for little children above the bright blue sky, a friend who will always love you a love that will not die.

I was seven years old, and was taken to the Baptist chapel by my grandmother who had virtually brought me up from birth. She had told me about Jesus, and as I started to join in with the words, it was as if The Lord had lifted me up onto His knee, just like the little girl in the picture on the chapel wall. The picture was entitled the hope of the world. I knew from this young age that this man Jesus, whom Gran had told me about, loved me. I walked down to the alter rail, the minister picked me up in his arms, and said. .

"When God opens your mouth, you will sing and glorify His name".

Coming out of the chapel I felt a new person and knew that God really loved me. I thought I could get through anything. I knew I had a friend for life and he would be with me forever. But first there would be many trials and hardships to go through.

My mother was a gamekeeper's daughter and one of seven, with three sisters and three brothers, she was the second youngest girl, and was born in Shropshire, but went to school in South Wales. Her father worked for the gentry, and was in much demand for his skills as a gamekeeper. After leaving Wales, the family moved to Grantley in Yorkshire for a while, and from there went to live at Harewood House Lodge. Eventually, they moved on again, this time taking up residence in Lincolnshire in the small village of Scawby. My grandfather had accepted a post as head gamekeeper to Lord Nelthorpe, along with his eldest son Eric, who was to act as under-gamekeeper, together with a man called Arthur Durnow, who was already employed there as an under-gamekeeper. After working there for several years, Grandfather lost his leg due to thrombosis, and had to give up game keeping altogether. From there the family moved to Ulceby in Lincolnshire, where he became landlord of the Yarborough Arms, the local public house. Mum had lots of men friends at the time and loved to be centre of attention. She had been engaged while she was in Scawby but had refused to marry her fiancé.

They were not to stay in Ulceby for long either, because Mum had fallen pregnant with me. At that time, in 1937 there was a great stigma attached to becoming pregnant out of wedlock, not only for the single mother, but it also brought shame on the whole family. Even before making plans to move, she had already got her eye on another man, he was a local chap and used to do a bit of work in the pub cellar. However, her mother being a very proud lady had already devised a plan to move quickly. So, it was up sticks and off again, this time to The Red Lion at Withern a little village just outside Louth. After they had moved; my mother was kept out of the way until it was time to give birth. This was so no one in the village would find out about the pregnancy.

My mother started in labour on 25th May 1938, and was taken to hospital by her brother, with a warning that after the birth she was to return home, alone. Mum had been seeing the cellar man at Ulceby for a while. After we moved, he still used to come on his motorbike to see her at the new pub. So when the baby was born [Me], his mother said they could take me to her house in Killingholme. I was taken to my new "grandmother's", who, as I grew older became a mother figure. Mary, her daughter, told me years later, that I had arrived in a wicker basket with nothing more than the clothes I had on.

Gran had been a widow two years by the time I arrived. She also lost a son around the same time, so she had a lot of love to give. I slept in her bedroom, with her and Mary. Frank, Mary's brother was in the small bedroom, whilst her other two brothers Chris and John, (who later became my father) slept in the middle bedroom. Mum and "Dad" got married by the time I was two. I was by this time feeling very secure with my gran; one day she sat me on her knee and told me that Mummy was going to have another baby. She was in hospital at that very moment giving birth. I didn't really understand, and besides, Gran was my mum, I was just glad my real Mother wasn't around. Anyway, Mum finally came out of hospital, and I found myself with a sister called Molly. So we had to make room for us all. I had been so happy with Gran and Aunt Mary. Mum, Dad, Molly and I, were moved into the biggest bedroom.

There was a sharp contrast between my mother's parents, and my dad's parents. They owned a fourteen-bed roomed hotel and were quite well placed, while Dad's had only a small link cottage with three bedrooms and were just ordinary country folk. Mum had to move in permanently now she'd had Molly, she didn't like it at all. When things didn't go right she always blamed me, telling me it was

3

my fault. She never said Molly had ruined her life it was always me. I always believed that Molly's dad was my dad. It wasn't until years later; I was to learn the truth.

Dad was offered a job in Sheffield, we all went with him, I was now three and a half and Molly was almost one. We were in rented accommodation in Sheffield when I became very ill. Mum told me I had a rash and would have to go to hospital. She told me that all I did was moan, as we were rushed through the streets. To add to the trauma, it was wartime and bombs were dropping and the sirens were wailing. We had to stop, in order to go into an air raid shelter. By the time we were allowed out of the shelter my condition had worsened considerably. Mum and Dad were arguing because he hadn't wanted to take me in the first place. When I eventually got into the casualty room a doctor diagnosed me as having spinal meningitis.

I couldn't remember much for a long time afterwards, but Mum told me two children had died, and three more had been left with complications such as, blindness and loss of limbs. She told me afterwards, that when I came out of hospital, I was a totally different little girl to the one who had gone in. I had brain damage, a cast in my right eye and could not walk properly. I suffered from a lot of head pain and constantly wet the bed, which didn't go down very well. I was put on a lot of medication. I can remember two new satin dresses; Mum must have bought me these when I came out of hospital.

We left Sheffield shortly after I came out of hospital. My days were very dark and dismal; this was a time in my life that I don't remember much about. My gran told me I was very slow in movement and thinking. I was very sleepy and tired, my head hurt continually, and I couldn't stand bright lights. I used to sit behind Gran to keep in the shade.

Dad and my two uncles were drinkers, but now they had started to drink a lot more. Aunt Mary and my gran kept the house going. Mum wasn't around very much; we never knew where she went. Dad wasn't long before he got work again and went off on his own. While Dad was away, Mum was always moaning about wanting a place of her own. At the other end of the village from us, there was an American army base, and on certain nights, we were put to bed early, so Mum could sneak out and go to the dances that they held there.

I was now five years old and it was time to start school. Aunt Mary used to take me, but school life for me started off badly. I was a quiet sickly child, and was unable to concentrate on one thing for very long. This didn't make me a great hit with most of the teachers. One day, the head-teacher, who hated me, whacked me around the head and dragged me out in front of the class. She asked if anyone wanted a lucky dip, (meaning me). She stated that, they wouldn't be getting much in this parcel. I was also being bullied regularly by other kids in the playground, because I always seemed to have a bad cough and runny nose, this seemed to give them the right to pick on me. One day I was being taunted by a group of kids, when a big girl called Hilda came to my rescue, the other kids seemed to respect her. I thanked her and she said.

"Don't worry they won't bother you again."
This was to be my first real friend. I found school very hard going, my lack of concentration was a

huge problem, especially with the main subjects like the three R's, [reading, writing, arithmetic.

Things were going from bad to worse at home, with Mum and Dad arguing all the time, the only peace in the house was when one of them went out. For much of the time we would be beaten with a belt, for minute things, sometimes for nothing at all. They beat us just to relieve their own anger. Mum's favourite saying whilst beating us, would be.

"No wonder people murder kids."

The only thing we were guilty of was having been born. We started to feel sorry for Dad, because as soon as he came home, we knew she would wind him up and start goading him. Dad used to work so hard to look after us all, but it was never good enough for Mum, she always wanted more. She wanted a house of her own and would compare our situation with the rest of her family, they all had their own homes, and we had nothing.

It was coming up to Christmas and Dad got a job away, this meant packing up and going with him into lodgings. This meant leaving Gran, Aunty Mary and my friend Hilda. Because the war was still on, the train was full of soldiers. It was a long journey and all I wanted to do, was reach our destination, Liverpool. We were jostled about as we searched the train looking for a seat. I can remember settling down on a ladies lap and falling asleep. When I awoke, we had already reached Liverpool. I was hurried off the train, still tired and very cold, it was snowing and it was very late at night.

Mum and Dad, hadn't had a civil word to say to each other the entire journey, and were still shouting on the platform. The stationmaster told us, we could wait in the waiting room, while Dad went to find us somewhere to stay. He had been gone for what seemed like an age. We were cold and hungry by the time he finally arrived, and were eventually taken off to our new temporary home. It was a long walk in the snow; all I wanted was to snuggle up to my gran. After being shown in to our new lodgings, which was an old Victorian house, with long wide steps leading up to the front door; Molly and I were taken straight upstairs to bed

Next morning I was taken off to my new school. I did painting and sewing, and kept myself to myself, and remained very quiet. We had been in Liverpool about six months, when Dad announced that we would be going home to see Gran for a week. I got very excited until, in the next breath, he told us we would be moving up to Scotland after our visit.

The week with Gran passed very quickly and before we knew it we were off again, this time to Ayrshire. It turned out to be a better move. We stayed with a lovely couple called, Mr & Mrs Parr. I really liked them and eventually started to love them as my own family. Of course, there was the inevitable new school I had to attend. Once again the bullying started because I couldn't read or write. To soften the blow, Dad let me go for dancing lessons. Mum and Dad were out a lot and we spent a lot of time with Grandpa and Grandma Parr, (as we had come to know them). As usual, it wasn't to last long. Uncle Chris rang and told Dad there were jobs for him back home, and they needed him to go. We didn't want to leave Scotland but Dad was a steel erector and had to go where the work was. Everybody wanted him for specialist jobs, which others wouldn't or couldn't do. People said he had nerves of steel to do some of the jobs he did.

We were back in Lincolnshire for a short while, then off again this time to Whitley bay. However, this was to be a bit different from the other times. Dad went off to work and we stayed with Mum's sister, in Knutsford. She and her husband had a butchers business in town. They had a Son my age, called Mike and we became good friends. They had another Son Ken, who was a lot older than Mike. He had joined the Chindits and was away in the war. I loved it at this place; we used to go swimming, and walking around the park with Aunty Flo and Mum. We had good food and were well looked after, it was one of the more memorable times of my young life.

Once again it was time to go back to Killingholme. We'd had a wonderful time in Knutsford and I thanked Aunty Flo for looking after us so well. I was going to miss her terribly.

As usual, we weren't to be home long before it was time to uproot again, this time to Garston, near Liverpool. When we arrived at our destination after a long journey, we were horrified at how dirty the house was, Mum wasn't very impressed, and she let Dad know in no uncertain terms, that she was not staying here. It was late though, so we went upstairs to bed anyway. Only to be awakened in the middle of the night by Mum putting the light on. To our horror, we found the room teeming with little red bugs. That was more than enough for Mum. Middle of the night or not we were not staying there. Instead, we went to the train station buffet, and stayed there until Dad found some better accommodation.

He eventually found us a place with a lovely family called the Kent's. Mrs Kent used to take us to Sefton Park, and we would sit near Peter Pans monument. She taught me to knit, and gave me lots of wool. I loved it and I knitted her a long scarf; it must have looked funny with all its different colours. She also encouraged me to start a scrapbook I loved her company. She and her husband reminded me of the Parr's in Scotland. We really got settled in there, and yes, I was found another new school. We were there a year, during which time the war had come to an end. There were big celebrations all over the country and the street parties in Liverpool were wonderful. When it was time to leave we were all very sad, but we thanked the Kent's for having us and for treating us so well.

We arrived back in Killingholme; it was wonderful to be home again at Grans. Once we had got settled back in, Mary and some of her friends took me to the Sunday school at the Baptist chapel. One day they were singing a hymn called, there's a friend for little children. As I looked around I saw a picture on the wall, called The Hope of the World. This was when I had a vision which was to become a reality. Things began to change in my life and I began to pray with Gran regularly.

The family next door to Gran's had a daughter called Mary, who used to babysit; she would read the bible to us at night. Often in the day we would go round to her house, and she would tell us stories from the bible. One day, she asked if I would like to be a bridesmaid for her older brother who was getting married. I couldn't wait to tell Gran. She took me round to Aunty Pat Dimbleby, who made my dress and hat. I was really excited, and it turned out to be a beautiful wedding. Just prior to the wedding, a tragedy happened. We used to go for walks with Mary Poole, one day when she was taking us home, she was feeling a bit poorly. Everyone was upset the next day, and I couldn't understand why? I was too happy and pre-occupied at the thought of being a bridesmaid. It wasn't until someone said that Mary had died, that I realised why people were so upset. They said she'd had a burst appendix; she was only sixteen. I felt sorry for Aunt Mary because, she was her best friend. Then I thought how wonderful it must be, to go to be with Jesus. But Mum soon brought me down to earth; she said that when people died they stank. This gave me horrible nightmares afterwards, and all I could think about was what Mum had said.

About this same time, Mum started on her quest to find a house of our own. It had to be said, we were a bit overcrowded to say the least. We had already had twenty-two different addresses and I wasn't quite ten. Mum put her name down for a council house; however, with the war just finishing priority was given to the ones who had been bombed out. Winter was once again upon us, and Mum had arranged for us to go into one of the empty billets, these buildings had been left by the vacating servicemen. They were long and roomy and many people were using them as homes. She began packing up our belongings we moved in and were now squatters.

Molly and I got excited when we found flushing toilets and wash hand basins. We had never seen a flushing toilet. We were only used to outside privies that the dilly men came to empty. We also had electricity, which made a change from trimming the wicks on the oil lamps. It felt like heaven, all these new fangled gadgets that didn't take much effort to make them work. It was certainly a lot easier for Mum. Dad got old army blankets and partitioned the room to separate us off from them. We ended up with three bedrooms, a living room and a kitchen. There was a coke-burning stove in the middle, which Mum had to cook on. We had a tin bath, a dolly tub to wash clothes in. Dad put up a swing for us to play on. We stayed for six months, but then the farmer who owned the land wanted to farm it again, so we had to move on.

We moved from there to another site at East Halton, where we were given a Nissan hut. It had a bathroom, two bedrooms and kitchen. Dad bought Molly and I a new bed; also a new one for Mum and himself. He also bought Mum a piano because she could play. She used to play in the pubs when they had a singsong, but whatever he did, it was still not good enough for her. The peace didn't last long they were at it again. The constant bickering and rows were getting worse, where would it all end? I wondered. How we all managed to struggle through those arguments is a mystery, but we did.

Molly and I really settled down in our new home, I remember Dad came home one day with a bike for each of us. We rode up and down the country roads, there wasn't a lot of traffic and we were safe on the roads then. One day Dad took us swimming in a pond near the abbey, which was close by. We took sandwiches and a drink, it was really good fun. When we had finished swimming Dad asked us what we would like to be when we grew up. I said.

"I would like to be a singer."

His eyes lit up and he said.

11

"Whatever you want to do in this life, you can achieve it if you're determined enough, when you reach eleven I will send you for singing lessons."

I was really excited on my eleventh birthday. I would soon be going to secondary school and all I wanted to do now was sing, paint and sew. I had failed my scholarship miserably; I just sat and wrote anything on the paper, it was like a foreign language to me. Molly on the other hand, was clever. She started going to whist drives with Mum. I would rather stay at home; I got more enjoyment playing with our cat. One day at school, our singing teacher, who didn't like me anyway; told the whole class that I couldn't sing and never would be able to. I was really hurt, because I knew deep down, that God had given me a talent for singing. I just knew she was wrong, and one day I would prove it

I started attending confirmation classes at church, in order to learn more about Christianity. I didn't tell anyone; I also went to pray for my friends, because my uncle Frank was doing awful things to them, and I thought that if I prayed, he would stop. I was still going to Gran's regularly and one day when I went, Frank was sitting with his head in his hands and crying. Mary was cross and Gran was upset. They didn't say anything to me but I knew something was badly wrong. The next day when I went round, I heard voices. I recognised the voice of the doctor. He was telling Gran that Frank was suffering from schizophrenia; all that was to me, was a long word. I did wonder what was wrong with Frank; after all he didn't look ill. I knew he used to do funny things like, staring at the wall all the time, and he used to eat eggs with the shells still on. He also drank heavily and hid his bottles all over the

12

place. He went out very late at night, nobody knew where or why. The doctor was saying that he had to be persuaded to go away voluntarily. Gran would have to sign a form to commit him to an asylum, but she refused point blank. She said she and Mary would look after him. I had a dream that night that Frank was putting Gran through a wringer, and I was helping her to escape. Frank's behaviour went steadily downhill

One day he had tipped his bed upside down and was underneath it. He also poured urine out of the chamber pot, all over the floor. On another occasion he went missing and everyone was out looking for him, but somehow he had managed to climb on top of the door, and was sat there, watching everyone else, looking for him. Dad used to go around at nights to try and talk to him, all to no avail.

Once, I decided to go to Gran's on my bike. Mum had told me not to go, because Frank was a danger to everyone, as well as to himself. Unbeknown to her, we sneaked off ignoring Mum's warning. The cycle felt heavy, but I loved it as I pushed against the wind. Going along the road, I saw a shadowy figure, half hidden in the bushes. I saw it was a man and he came towards me. I saw that his trousers were undone. I started to push harder on the pedals I had to get passed. He started after me and tried to grab me. I was terrified; everything seemed to be going into slow motion. I somehow managed to keep ahead of him, he was shouting and swearing.

When I finally reached Gran's, I banged on the door to be let in; Gran asked what on earth the matter was. I was too shaken and breathless to speak, so she gave me a small glass of brandy. When I had settled down, she again asked me what had happened. I told her what Frank had done. Mary started shouting at me and called me a liar.

"Frank wouldn't do that." She shouted again. "You are a liar."

Gran told me to go home; the incident was never mentioned again. Not long after, I was out with my friends. Frank came up to us and threw a handful of money on the floor.

"You know what that's for." He said to my friend. She was only nine, and he just laughed at her.

Gran's household was in turmoil. Dad tried to talk to him again, but in the end Gran gave in, and signed the papers to commit him. He was placed in Bracebridge Heath in Lincoln, in a secure unit for the mentally ill. It broke Gran's heart. Dad went nearly every day to see him. Once he took me, I can always remember Dad and Mum having a big row over it, because she said it wasn't a place to take young children. I will never forget that experience. There were people just walking round all over, with this vacant look on their faces. They looked as if they didn't belong to the body that was being dragged around. It wasn't until years later, I found out they were drugged up to keep them quite. We really loved Uncle Frank deep down, why did he have two sides to him?

Mum got worse and started telling Dad that he should be in Lincoln with his mad brother. I asked Mum not keep rowing, but they got worse, and the rows would be followed by hours of silence. Mum would goad Dad all the more. I didn't know which was worse. But we knew when he'd had enough; he would go white with temper and then hit her.

14

Even this didn't stop her; it got so bad that Molly and I would get thrashed, just because we were there. We tried to keep out of the way as much as possible, but it wasn't easy, as it became an every waking hour occurrence. Molly would go to her friend Joyce's, she lived near us and she would spend hours there, just to keep out of the way. I would just wander about for hours, until it was nearly bedtime.

Mum decided to go out to work; she went potato picking and pea pulling. This made Dad mad because, he said it was his job to bring the money in and she was to clean the house, and cook the meals. This didn't deter her though and at the weekends we even went with her. Molly enjoyed it but I hated it and went to chapel on a Sunday instead

One-day Mum came home very excited; we had been allocated a house in Killingholme. Dad refused to go. So one day while he was at work, Mum packed up our belongings and moved us to our new house. It was great; Molly and I had our own bedroom. Dad was very angry when he found out what Mum had done. His anger wasn't to last long though when he realised how happy Molly and I were. He knew that we were all better off in the new house, than squashed up with Gran. As usual things weren't to last, their rows started all over again, eventually Mum came to sleep in my bedroom. They began to go their separate ways, Mum would go her way and Dad went his, both would come home late at night; usually drunk.

I was doing well at school, but I felt so lonely without my friend Hilda. Once more the other kids would pick on me. My art teacher felt sorry for me and would let me stay in the class at playtimes. This was to benefit me greatly, because I actually gained top marks in art and needlework. I also joined the choir and was given the job of secretary for the drama club. We presented many plays and after they heard me sing; they let me perform all the solo parts. Dad was very proud and found me a singing teacher from the Methodist church, called Percy Thompson. He had trained Cathleen Ferrier.

Mum got worse, Molly and I were both fed up with her, she was always out late with other men, and everyone seemed to know but Dad. She once went to stay with her parents for six months, saying she needed a break. She just left without a word or thought for Molly or me. When she did come home, nothing had changed; she arrived home unannounced, at three in the morning. Dad had locked the doors but Molly sneaked down and let her in. When Dad called us in the morning, he was so angry; I hid Mum in the wardrobe. I didn't know what to say to him, so she stayed there until he went to work.

After she emerged from the wardrobe, there was a big row between Mum and Mary. Mary had been looking after us while she had been away. Dad also found out the name of the man she had been seeing behind his back, but she denied everything. I think she was incapable of telling the truth.

Mum had only been home a couple of days, and we were sat having dinner. Molly was out as usual, Dad asked Mum to pass him a spoon, as she was sitting near the cutlery draw. She answered by saying.

"Get your own bloody spoon."

He looked at her and his face turned white with temper. I feared the worst this time. He threw a cup of hot tea; I had to duck to avoid it hitting me before it hit Mum. He said,

"Get me a f...... spoon." She replied.

"That was a manly thing to do; you should be locked up with your mad brother."

That did it; he threw a big mug at her, hitting her on the head. It smashed on impact, knocking her glasses from her face. I bent down to pick them up, blood was everywhere, and it was streaming down her face. I got one of her aprons and put it onto the cuts; I didn't know what to do. Dad just sat there as if nothing was wrong. I told her to get up we needed help, we went to the next-door neighbours. I had to lead her she couldn't see for all the blood.

When we got to Rubie's, she wasn't in. I was panicking, I had to get her somewhere; it was difficult; not many people liked Mum. I knocked on Jennie's door, but she told me she wanted nothing to do with it. I begged her to help or she might die. Jennie's husband let us in and he called for The Doctor. We put a large towel around Mum's head. The doctor wasn't long before he came; he had to put thirteen stitches in the wound, after taking all the pieces of pot out first. What a terrible sight, there was blood everywhere; all along the road, up the neighbour's paths, I was covered in it too. When the doctor had finished, he asked me to sit with her whilst he went to see my father. I was so frightened, I suggested to my Mum that we run away, but she said.

"We can't, we have no-where to go."

I couldn't tell Gran, she had enough to think about with Frank being in Lincoln. The doctor finally came

17

back from speaking to Dad, but he hadn't got anywhere. He told us, Dad had said he was not sorry and would do it again, and told the doctor to mind his own business. The doctor's advice to Mum was to leave and get a divorce

After the doctor left; Mum just said. "Come on Joan, let's go home."
I wanted to scream, no I am not going home, but nothing came out. As we approached the door of the house, I thought maybe when Dad saw her, he would be sorry, but when we got inside, he wasn't, and said it would be worse next time. I couldn't believe what he had done, whilst were out of the house, he had scrubbed everywhere spotless, not a drop of blood in sight. Mum was still as white as a sheet. There was no emotion showing on Dad's face as he pushed past us and went to bed. Mum looked at herself in the mirror. I thought she was going to cry. But she just picked up her glasses and went to bed. Mum, Molly and I, all slept in my room Dad never did say he was sorry, and the fighting continued.

I loved my school despite being constantly picked on; it was better than being at home. I also started to go to the tin mission where they showed films. I met a new friend called Rose, her mum and family were really nice and I stayed there as much as possible. After all, Mum and Dad didn't care where we were. I got my dinner and bank money on a Monday, and they didn't see much of me until Friday. At the weekends I would go to my singing teacher in Grimsby, he was very good and informed me I was a mezzo-soprano, and could reach seven octaves. This didn't mean much to me at that time. He was a Methodist lay preacher too and he used to take me and other pupils round the Methodist circuit. We performed concerts all over the county. But I couldn't concentrate the way I should have done because of the troubles at home.

Dad had caught Mum with other men on more than one occasion, he would throw her out; she would leave for a few days and then come back home again. We didn't know where she was or whom she was with. She would send me to go to the post office to pick up her mail, where she had a special box. The letters were all from married men. She said it was to be our secret and I was not to tell Dad, otherwise, he would get angry and kill us both. I don't know how he found out that I knew but he came home one day and called me a filthy liar. He threw Mum out of the door beating her as she went. Then he turned and began to thrash me saying,

"Liar, I will never trust you again."

He also beat up the man she had been seeing; still she denied it all saying.

"We're just friends."

This time Mum stayed away for two months. I decided there and that when I got married I would stick to my husband no matter what.

2

I was now coming up to fourteen, and decided I would start going out at nights to meet people. We only had to ask Dad and he would give us money just to get rid of us. I started to go to the village dances; it was at one of these dances that I met Alan. He was eighteen and quite drunk but that didn't seem to bother me. I was used to folk being drunk. I had been brought up with it. I was besotted with him, he asked me to meet him at the dance the following week. I was excited at the thought of seeing him again, and after choir practise I went to meet him. He gave me some beer to drink, but I didn't like the taste so I drank it as quickly as I could. The feeling it gave me was good and seemed to give me more confidence.

Following that night, I was on cloud nine, especially when he asked me if I wanted to go to the police ball with him. I felt all grown up. We agreed; I would meet him there the following Friday night. But I felt I needed to see him before Friday, so in the evenings I used to sneak out of the house and go to his village. One night Dad came looking for me because I had missed my piano lesson. I was with Alan when he shouted.

"Is that you Joan?" I answered.

"Yes, and this is Alan."

I could see that old familiar grim look come over Dad's face.

"Alan bloody who?" he said.

Dad immediately dropped his bike and went for Alan, but he got onto his motorbike and rode off.

When I got home I told Mum what had happened, she said.

"Don't worry, I will cover for you in the future, if you will continue going to the post office for my mail."

I didn't think of what the consequences might be after the last time, I just wanted to see Alan. So I did what she asked.

On the Friday night, I went with Alan to the police ball and I told them I was sixteen. The dance was a disaster; I drank much too much and ended up outside being sick. I must have passed out; because when I came to, Alan was slapping my face, in an effort to bring me round. He ended up taking me home to his mum's house and I slept with his two sisters. I wasn't worried about Dad, because Mum had already told him I was sleeping at a friend's house for the night. When I went home the next day, I dare not say a word to anyone. I felt really poorly, but didn't realise, that it could be put down to the amount of drink I had consumed

The local preacher asked me to be a Sunday school teacher, but I was so wrapped up in Alan, I told him I didn't have the time to train. My singing teacher told me I was too young to be courting; I should concentrate on my singing and other gifts, but I only wanted to be with Alan.

When I left school, I got an apprenticeship to train as a dressmaker. This was at a very high-class workroom at the back of a lady's house called, Madam Bellamy. I would earn seventeen shillings a week. It meant a seven-mile bike ride, early in the morning, in all weathers, to the train station. Dad helped me with a lot of my sewing, he had learnt to be a tailor when he was fourteen, but had given it up to go contracting. He bought me a treadle sewing machine, and I started to do alterations at home. I also used to make Gran's dresses.

Alan bought himself a new motorbike, and Dad condescended to let him come and pick me up at the house. Dad didn't seem to mind so much now, even though I had just had my fifteenth birthday.

I met a lady at Madam Bellamy's; she used to pop in for a few things now and again. Her name was Brenda and she was telling me her husband had multiple sclerosis; they had a ten year old son called Stephen. Charlie her husband hadn't worked since he was twenty-five, which meant she was the breadwinner. She managed to get me a job singing in a workingmen's club, which paid me thirty shillings a night. After my Saturday morning singing lesson, I would go over to Brenda's house and stay for the weekend. Alan used to come over on his motorbike, and we would all go to the club together. There was an agent in the club one night; he told me he could get me bookings for other clubs.

Brenda saw me off from her house the following Monday morning. I rode my bike to the station at Grimsby and caught the train to Habrough. After riding the four miles home, I put my cycle down and walked in the back door, singing this is my lovely day. Dad was waiting fist clenched; he started beating me. I dropped my music case and ran to the front room. I managed to get the door bolted before he could get to me. To my horror, his fist came clean through the door. I knew at this point my jaw was broken, and my teeth were bleeding badly. Dad was shouting all sorts of abuse, saying I had been out with different men and telling all sorts of lies. I tried to explain where I had been, but he had gone too far to even listen. He came into the room and repeatedly punched me in the back. I managed to break away from him and ran out the door for fear of my life. I stood in the middle of the road wondering where to turn. He was still shouting when the lady who ran the post office pulled up in her car. She could see there was something was dreadfully wrong, and told me to get into the car. She took me to her house and sent for the doctor who tended my wounds. The next day I went back home for my case. Dad had said that I would be back, and that wherever I went, he would find me and bring me back home. I said I would never return home again. Even to this day, I have never found out why he beat me so badly.

I ended up going to Brenda's; she gave me one of her bedrooms and told me I could stay as long as I pleased. I had been there about three weeks when she took in another girl, called Diane, we used to joke that we were foster sisters. Di went to work with Bren. She came from a family with nine children, her parents were both alcoholics, hence her reason for leaving home. I told Gran I had left home because Mum and Dad were always fighting. Molly also left and went to live with her friend in the village.

Alan came one day and asked if I wanted to go to Belgium, with a friend and his girlfriend. I said.

"Yes."

I couldn't hide my excitement at going abroad for a holiday. I told Alan I wanted to meet his friends, to get to know them before we went. He arranged for us all to go out together one night. They were called Charlie and Glenda, I thought at the time what a nice couple they were.

When we arrived in Belgium, I got a job singing at the White Horse Inn. It was after one of my gigs, that Alan said Charlie had suggested swapping girlfriends for the night. I was shocked that Alan would ever think of anything like that, never mind actually asking me. During one of my nights of singing I drank two bottles of wine. I don't know why, maybe I was disgusted at what had been suggested. The owner of the inn knew there was something wrong, and offered me a job as resident singer but I refused; I was so confused, I didn't know what to do. He said the offer was there if I wanted to change my mind.

After we arrived home, I never saw Charlie and Glenda again. I asked Alan what the hell it had all been about; he just snubbed me and said.

"Forget it."

I decided there and then, that I had to finish with him. I gave him back the engagement ring he had given me. Brenda kept begging me to take him back, stressing that it was only one incident and I shouldn't let it spoil things. After much persuasion, I finally agreed. Shortly after this Alan and I started making our wedding plans. I was on cloud nine once again. After all the trouble we'd had at home and everything else, I thought at last things were going to be different. I was now eighteen years old and I had been engaged to Alan for two years, it was time to get married. I really appreciated Brenda's input and help, especially as my own mother wasn't around

It was in the middle of making my wedding arrangements, when Molly decided to run away to London with her boyfriend, to live with his mother.

Mum had left Dad to live and work in a hotel as a silver service waitress. Which wasn't going to be very helpful to my plans, but we carried on without them

During this time we went to stay in Cardiff with Alan's brother and his wife for a holiday, I entered a talent contest in the Kenard ballroom Cardiff. I sang three songs two of Shirley Bassey's, they ask me to sing every night for the remainder of our stay and when it was time to leave they offer me a contract, but I had to turn it down because of my upcoming marriage

I was now earning a lot of money, singing in clubs all over Lincolnshire. I was becoming well known. I was known as Grimsby's Shirley Bassey. My singing teacher didn't like it, and said the songs I was singing were rubbish. I was still singing sacred songs with the modern ones, but I had stopped going to church because, the money was more important to me than God. Every week, I would hand over my wages to Alan to put away for our wedding. Alan worked for his father on the farm and earned five pounds a week. On a good week I could earn twenty pounds a week plus. I started to buy all sorts of little bits and pieces for our bottom drawer. I used to take Charlie on the train to Killingholme to visit Gran and Mary, I was always busy, but Charlie liked to get out a bit

As I was only eighteen, I needed to get permission from Dad to get married. After much coaxing and pleading he agreed to sign. Although he would never go to church, Gran managed to talk him round and eventually he agreed to give me away. Alan's dad put his wages up to seven pounds a week. He took me to look at a small cottage on the farm, and showed me how he had decorated it, I thought it was fantastic. Alan's mum bought us a settee, an armchair, a bedroom suite and a sideboard. Dad gave us a piano, it was wonderful, all I could have hoped for. I would now be my own boss, or so I thought.

We had our wedding in Grimsby at All Saint's Church. Molly came up from London to be my Chief Bridesmaid. Alan's sister Carol and Diane were my other two Bridesmaids. Brenda and I had made all the dresses and Brenda arranged the reception at her house. On the morning of the wedding I went to see Charlie, he was unable to go to the wedding because it would be too much for him. Charlie said.

"You know you shouldn't marry him, it will only end in tears."

It was all that I wanted, so I didn't take any notice. Besides, everyone was waiting at the church. It was only whilst I was waiting for the car to take us to the church, that I thought about Charlie's words. Anyway, it was too late, I was too afraid of the consequences to call it off. The car arrived for dad and me; I didn't go see Charlie again. I got into the car and everyone came out to see me off. I went into the church and went through with the ceremony. When it was over, I was sure that God would make it work for me. From that moment on, I must have been wearing rose tinted glasses.

We had the reception; and after saying goodbye to all our friends, we picked up our cases and headed off to the train station. Everyone came to see us off. Alan had booked us a honeymoon in Cromer. It was only when we were on the train that I suddenly realised; I had left the hotel booking confirmation on my dressing table. I just knew Alan would be very angry. So I pushed it to the back of my mind, I knew the hotel name and knew it was on the sea front. I would leave it and say nothing until we got there. Alan was up tight already, we'd had one delay with the train being late, so I thought keep your mouth shut; wait for him to calm down.

Then came the moment I was dreading, I had to tell him what I had done, he called me dumb and stupid. He was making so much noise as we got off at the station; the guard put us in the ticket office, until he had sorted everyone else out. Within an hour we got a taxi, it was a twenty-mile drive to Cromer. All the way Alan just got angrier and angrier and shouting asked.

"What's the name of the hotel?"

I sat and said nothing the whole journey. Fortunately for me, the driver knew the hotel we were going to. Alan told him what was going on and how thick and stupid I had been. We arrived at the hotel 12.30am, only to find it locked. We rang the bell and the lady remembered our booking and showed us to our room. She said.

"The formalities will do in the morning."

All Alan did was moan about what had gone on, he grumbled about the journey, grumbled about the room. I just laid there and listened, until I dropped off to sleep

I remember thinking dejectedly to myself, what a wonderful part of my life this is. I awoke next morning to find him already up and dressed.

"Come on." He said.

"Get dressed we'll go for a walk, we have missed breakfast while you've being asleep."

I was hoping we could go to the beach to avoid asking him for any money. He had all the money and that's how it was going to be for the rest of our married life. After all, he thought he could manage it better than me. I was feeling brave, after we'd had a swim; I asked if I could have some money to buy Charlie and Brenda a small present. As soon as I opened my mouth I knew I'd made a big mistake.

"Bloody money for presents, we haven't got enough for ourselves, never mind that bloody lot."
As we were walking past a shop he gave me some small change.

"Buy some postcards, it will have to do." He said.
The whole week was all so disappointing, not like the honeymoon I'd dreamt of. No romance, everything taken for granted, just like he owned me body and soul. I was his now, to own and do as he pleased with.

I remember on the last night of our honeymoon, he took me for a meal to a Chinese restaurant. When we arrived he started to poke fun at the waiters, calling them foreigners and saying they shouldn't be in our country. I felt so ashamed and embarrassed, I couldn't eat my meal, when he had finished; he paid the waitress and called me an ungrateful bitch; just to show me up once again in front of others.

I went back to the hotel on my own. When he returned later, having been drinking, he asked.

"What is the matter with you?"
I explained what had upset me; he told me it had been a joke, but he was the only one laughing. The next morning on the way to the train, he let me buy some small presents to take back home. Charlie's words came flooding back, and I wondered what sort of life lay in front of me. Maybe this was a one

off I reasoned, and he would change when we got settled.

When we got home to our cottage I was convincing myself, that I hadn't made a mistake after all, and that things would be all right. I went up to our bedroom to get changed. On seeing my wedding dress hanging on the back of the door, tears welled up inside me; I knew deep in my heart that I had made a big mistake. I brushed the thoughts to one side and wrapped the dress up in a sheet, and put it away in the cupboard. Alan had made it quite clear that he didn't want any children.

"I have enough with you." He'd say.

So I decided to get a job in a shoe shop three days a week, I also helped in the fields, especially at harvest time. I learnt to plough the fields and the milk cows. I didn't have enough time hardly to turn around. Alan spent most of his time in the pub;

I went to church on Sunday's and I joined the women's institute. I was still doing a lot of singing at the weekends, but as usual Alan got all the money. The only money I was allowed; was the rent and food money. I never got anything extra. He kept the money in a tin on the sideboard, but warned me not to touch it or I would regret it. I can only assume he meant I would get a beating. Although at that time he never said this outright. I also had to have his meal hot and ready on the table, if it was a bit late, or he came in late and it was cold, he would get angry and banging his fist on the table, would shout.

"This is my house and you will live by my rules, if you know what's good for you."

[I wondered just what was good for me]. We had by now been married two years.

All my friends were having their first babies; I dared to mention to Alan that I would like to have one. His comment was.

"We wouldn't have a life with a brat to look after."
I didn't have much of a life to speak of anyway. He used to tell everyone how happy we were, which pleased my Dad. Molly had come home from London and gone to live with a girl called Maxine, which certainly hadn't pleased him at all. She had left her boyfriend in London because she found out he was having an affair. He wasn't bothered about her; he just put her on a train and told her to go home. After all she was only a dumb blonde from the country. Molly wouldn't go out much after that, even when Alan's brother asked her out no strings, she just wouldn't go. Eventually, she went back to live with Dad, she even went to stay with Mum for a while; Mum had got a job as a housekeeper for a big businessman. Molly was still hurting and wouldn't entertain the thought of any man for a long while after that.

3

A short while after we were married, Alan's dad became ill and died shortly afterwards. He had left Alan two thousand pounds in his will. Alan gave me the cheque and asked me to put it into the bank; Mum was convinced that he would be treating me, once the cheque had cleared. However, the money wasn't mentioned again until, one day when he announced, that he was going to buy some pigs and set up his own business

This kept him out the house more, so in order to give Brenda a break, I used to bring Charlie over for visits a couple of days a week. His condition was getting worse and it made it harder for Bren to cope and go to work as well. Dad had refused to let me take Charlie to his house; he said.

"We might catch something from him."

Charlie was always happy despite his progressive illness; he was always saying that God was going to heal him. His favourite saying was.

"Never fear, God will provide sufficient for today."

Brenda just used to laugh. I would have loved to have Charlie's faith at that time. Alan didn't like Charlie or Bren, calling them scroungers; we had many a row about it. He wouldn't do anything to help, he said.

"He's your friend, get on with it."

When I had the bookings, Alan would take me to the clubs at weekends, mostly to make sure he got the money. I asked him again one night, about having children but again he said he had enough on with me. I was now nineteen. Life was getting very difficult because now, I no longer had Charlie

31

to confide in. He was the only one who knew how tough my life was with Alan. I knew he wouldn't discuss it with anyone, not even Brenda. Unfortunately, due to his illness, Charlie was finding it harder to move away from the house, and I missed him.

A year had passed and I felt some changes occurring in my body so I went to the doctors. I was a bit frightened, having had so much illness in the past. I couldn't understand what was happening to me. I was over the moon when he told me I was pregnant. I was sure that this would change Alan. I couldn't wait to spread the news. The first person I told was Alan's mum. I thought this would be a nice surprise and buck her up; it had only been six months since her husband died. I asked her how many babies she had wanted?

"None." She replied.

"I only had them because that's what he wanted."
I couldn't wait to tell Alan, I was so excited, I just blurted out the news. He got very cross and said.

"You fool, that's the biggest mistake and the most idiotic thing you have done so far."

I was physically worn out during my pregnancy. I was so naïve; they gave me books to read because, I didn't even know how babies were born. Carol my sister-in-law, was the only one who was pleased for me, and turned out to be a real blessing. She even reprimanded Alan for his attitude towards me, but it didn't make any difference, he still wouldn't accept it. He would not lie near me in bed; he said when the baby moved it made him feel sick. I had a very traumatic nine months, not knowing quite what to expect. Mum didn't even come to see me. I couldn't have Charlie to talk to, so I spent a lot of time with Carol. During my pregnancy, my sister Molly had met and married a man named George. They had fallen for a baby as soon as they were wed. I was really pleased for her after all the trouble she had gone through in her last relationship with her former fiancé.

I was really ill whilst carrying the baby and Alan couldn't bear to come near me. To humiliate me further, he would make me walk naked around the bed. Telling me how grotesque I looked and what an awful shape I was. My wedding vows were to love and obey. The degradation continued; I didn't know what to do. He was mocking and laughing at me all the time. Carol had to send for the doctor, because I was getting awful pains in my stomach, I became very poorly. Two weeks later I was in the hospital. Alan refused to take me, so Carol volunteered instead. Alan told me, he would see me when I'd had it, when I looked a better shape to be seen with.

Well this was it; Carol saw me into the hospital and told me she would see me after the baby was born. The doctor came and examined me but the pains had stopped. I believed they were going to operate, because I thought that was how you had babies. I really wished Gran or Bren could have been there, just to explain to me what was going on. The doctor looked worried, he told me I was a month overdue, my pelvis was too small; and I would have to have an induction. He told the nurse the baby was struggling and that the heartbeat was getting weaker. I asked the nurse how babies were born.

"The same way it got in there in the first place dear." She said. After three days of pain and a drip in my arm the doctor finally announced.

"You have a baby girl but she is very poorly."
They had to put a tube down her throat to get her breathing. I heard the nurse say she was well overdue, because the umbilical cord was rotten. She weighed eight pounds, eight ounces. They were still fighting to make my beautiful, dark haired little girl breath. Suddenly there was a sigh of relief from everyone, as she gave out a little cry.

"She's going to be O.K." The doctor said.
I was so relieved.

Alan's mum came that night; she was excited about the baby. She said Alan wouldn't come; he had gone to the pub to wet the babies' head. He actually managed a visit three days after the baby had been born; his comments were.

"When do they start to look human, you have got yourself a handful now."
While I was in the hospital, I made friends with the girl in the next bed. Her name was Madge and her husband was called Ted. Ted had been coming to visit Madge since the day she was brought in, and I thought how good that was. We became good friends from then on. Madge confided in me a few months later, saying that she thought I was a single mum because Alan had not come to see me, the way her husband had come to see her. In those days, we were taught how to wash and bath our babies on the ward before we were allowed to go home. They were taken into the nursery at night to enable us to rest and sleep. Four weeks later, I was allowed home, and Carol came to collect me, not Alan.

The church I was attending at the time, was open as we passed by on our way home, so I went in and thanked God for a safe delivery. This was called being "churched"; a lot of new mums were expected to do this at that time. The vicar said to me.

"You would think you were the only young Mum there is."

I felt that I was.

"Well done." He said. "Have you decided on a name for her?"

"Lesley." I said. "But I will have to consult Alan first."

We arranged the Christening would be in two weeks time. The vicar prayed for us before we left, by the time we arrived home, Pauline, who was Carol's sister had cleaned up and got the water on.

I was breast-feeding and was told to rest in the afternoons. However, I found difficult to get a rest with no one to help me. The district nurse came three times a week, to see that every thing was O.K. After coming out of the hospital with the baby, I got a small dog and called her Judy, she became a real good friend. When the baby was outside in her pram, she would bark to let me know when the baby was awake. I told Alan I wanted to call the baby Lesley.

"Over my dead body, that's a boy's name." He said.

Well we will have to think of a name soon because I have booked the Christening for next week. He said.

"She will be called Kay."

When I told Brenda what we were going to call her, she laughed and said.

"You might as well just call her A, B, or C."

Kay was Christened at eight weeks old, by this time I was exhausted, but no! According to Alan, I was fit enough to help with the milking, do the housework and get meals ready

"That's what women are for, stop grumbling." He said.

All Alan ever did, was go to work, come home, get his tea, then go to the pub. Kay seemed to cry all the time; this made things much worse between Alan and me. When he came home from the pub, he would get angry because she was crying and he couldn't get to sleep. Kay was crying franticly one morning, so I got out of bed, and rang the doctor. He came out straightaway, examined her and said.

"You did well to call me when you did; she's very close to having pneumonia."

She was very poorly so he arranged for the nurse to come in everyday. The doctor also noticed that her tongue was fixed to the bottom of her mouth. Which was the reason why she was always hungry; she couldn't get her milk properly, hence the continual crying? I told Alan, but he couldn't cope with illness. According to him it was an inconvenience and slowed him up, he didn't have time to deal with it. I'd had her it was down to me.

I constantly had to see the doctor and when Kay was six months old, I had to have surgery to my womb. I still didn't know where I stood with Alan; one day he would come in from work angry, the next he would be O.K. I had to approach him with caution all the time, to see what sort of mood he was in. After I came home from hospital and began to pick up a bit; I started to go out singing again to help with the finances. Alan went out and bought three breeding sows and a hundred egg laying chickens. He had also started drinking heavily, mainly because we now had the extra money coming in. I didn't tell anyone that he was taking all the money I was earning, and spending it on drink. According to Alan, I wasn't allowed money; I didn't need it

Kay was nine months old and finally I'd had enough. I started to pack my clothes to leave. Alan was furious, he didn't want me to take Kay; but I did anyway. I had told Molly what I was going to do. I told her everything about the money, the way he treated me and the physical abuse I'd suffered, not to mention the verbal abuse and how he used to discuss our sex life in front of his mates. Molly said I was a fool to stay, she said to go and live with her, and then I could keep the money I earned. I told her about the letter the doctor had written to Alan, telling him how he should leave me alone sexually for a while; how he had torn the letter up, and forced me to have sex anyway. The pain was excruciating. He seemed to thrive on hurting me and causing me pain. This created a great deal of physical damage, which resulted in me having to have another op, whilst I was at Molly's.

When I next saw Mum, she told me to go home and work at my marriage; I thought, that's good advice coming from you. Molly got milk fever and I helped her husband George to look after her. George was so good to Molly; it made me realise, watching the two of them together, just how bad Alan really was. I'd thought that my marriage was

37

going to be like theirs. Shortly after this, I had talks with Alan and his mum; he assured me that things would be different if I would go back to him, so in the end, I decided to give it another try. However, when I got home I found things weren't any better; in fact it was quite the reverse. He still put demands on me for sex, how he wanted to do it etc., depending on his mood at the time.

Alan had many friends both in the pub and at the local hunt meetings. A young girl named Jane had just got married, and lived in a caravan at the rear of the pub. Jane was nineteen and had a lot to do with the hunt; it was her father that Alan had bought the pigs from. He used to take the pigs to Jane's farm, to have them serviced by their boar, so he got to know her very well. I thought I had caught Alan and Jane holding hands once, but dismissed it from my mind. One day Jane came to me crying, she had a black eye. She told me that Rob, her husband, had done it. I felt sorry for her and took her into the house. I put Kay to bed, and gave Jane my last cigarette. She eventually said, she would go back home. I went to look for Alan to tell him what had happened. Jane had been gone about ten minutes by the time I found him. I couldn't believe my eyes. They were in the barn, and they were kissing. When I asked what the hell was going on? He told me, he was comforting her because she was crying. He said he wasn't kissing her, I was imagining it. I found out later that they had been having an affair for quite a while. This had been the reason for the beating she had received from Rob; they later divorced.

I couldn't believe Alan could do this to me, after all his promises. Kay was ten months old, I didn't say another word about it, I decided to leave him again and go to Molly's. I started to pack our belongings, but Alan came in and caught me, he told me that if I left, I had to leave Kay with him. I pushed the pram to the bus stop, but he made me get on the bus without her.

"How can you do this?" I said.

He just ignored me and walked away, taking Kay with him. When I got to Molly's, she suggested that I get settled in and then get a job; then go get Kay. I didn't know what to do? I couldn't think straight never mind get a job.

Bernard, a friend of Alan's, had known about the affair and had told Alan in no uncertain terms, that he didn't agree with it. He knew Alan kept me without money and one day he came round to Molly's house, he handed her an envelope with some money in it. I was unable to eat or sleep, all I wanted, was to go home to Kay. I constantly rang the farm to ask him about her, but he refused to come to the phone. Molly told me I was stupid to keep on ringing him. After a week of constantly ringing the pub, they made him come to phone. I asked him how Kay was, but he told me she didn't want to see me. I cried down the phone and begged him to let me see her. He eventually brought her to Molly's some time later. I was so pleased to see her. I couldn't believe what terrible things he said next. He said to Kay.

"This is your whore of a Mother; she doesn't want you and didn't even come to see you on your birthday."

This really rocked me, I was speechless, Kay looked at me and took three steps towards me; I started to cry.

"Look." Alan said to her.

"She can cry faster then she can pee."

"Please can I come home and try again?" I said.

"If you come home it's on my terms." He replied.

I had no choice; I needed to be with Kay.

"If you come home you can have two and sixpence a day, all the other money you earn, I'll have it, and most of all you'll do as I say."

"You are stupid to let him tell you what to do." Molly said.

I agreed anyway, and went back home.

I was only home a few months when I fell pregnant with our second child. I was really happy, once again, I thought this would change Alan for the better, but I was mistaken he still went his own selfish way. He wouldn't let me have any responsibility; he did all the shopping and paid all the bills. He even told me what to cook for dinner everyday. I didn't ask any questions, I just did as I was told. He would stay out all night, come home and get ready for work. I didn't say anything to anyone. I was just pleased to be in my little cottage with Kay. I did the gardening, all of the decorating and made all Kay's clothes. Any free time I managed to get, I would spend oil painting. I had even started making clothes for the new baby, I was sure it would be another girl.

The doctor was pleased with my progress, but I had to have injections three times a day. Alan didn't notice how ill I was, or more to the point, didn't even care; as long as it didn't interfere with his routine. Again he wouldn't come near me, especially when the baby moved; once again he said it made him feel sick. My weight increased dramatically from nine stones to thirteen. I couldn't wait to go into the home and have my baby. I was putting out some rubbish one day and fell and broke my ankle. I prayed.

"Please God let my baby be alright." I was in agony.

Alan agreed to take me shopping one day, but I couldn't cope with it, I felt really ill. So, he decided I ought to go to the hospital. Once again he left me with Carol and went home.

Some of the husbands were sitting with their wives in the waiting room, and although Carol was with me I felt so alone. Eventually the nurse came to me and Carol went home. I knew I was overdue and got frightened when they told me they would have to use the drip again. I was really suffering with pains in my back; I was on and off the bed all the time. They gave me an injection and I slept for a while. The doctor came when I awoke and told me I was in labour. I was waiting for the nurse to come with the drip; then I saw her. I stood up and there was an almighty crash, my waters broke and just flooded everywhere. I had one big pain and the nurse shouted for someone to get the trolley. She said the babies' head was already in full view, twenty minutes later I'd had my son Peter. With nothing more than two labour pains, no bother at all. I was both shocked and amazed it had happened so fast. All the nurses came to see him, because he had been born so quickly. I was overjoyed; I thought this would definitely change things, now that Alan had a son.

The nurse said she would ring Alan to tell him the news. She told me I was to rest until he came to visit. The nurse took Peter to the nursery; he had long black curly hair. I just wanted to go home and show him to his dad. Alan sent a message back saying he couldn't get in to visit, it was harvest time and he was too busy. Peter was three days old by the time Alan came to see us. I was desperate to get home; I had missed Kay's birthday again by being in the home.

On my way home with Pauline, once again I stopped at the church to give thanks to God for our Son's safe arrival. I asked God to make me a better person and give me a happy family. I was convinced Alan would become more of a family man now he had a son, but I found life harder than ever. Kay was taking time to toilet train properly. On top of everything else Alan insisted I started singing again. He said we needed the money now we had another brat to feed. Brenda said.

"You need to slow down and rest a bit you have just had a baby.

We had two good friends called Val and Keith; Alan had suggested we go to Butlins for a holiday, just the four of us. I wanted to take the children but he wouldn't hear of it, he said his mother would look after the kids. I was a bit wary about going after the episode on the last holiday, but I knew I could trust Val. I said I didn't want to leave the kids, but in the end I agreed and Alan made the booking.

Alan used to go to a nearby town called Barton; he had been out one night and woke me up when he came home. He said he wanted to talk to me; He asked if I would like to go to a party with him? It seemed he didn't really want to take me, because I was dull and boring. Apparently though, he had been asked to take me to meet his friends, and to cheer me up. Christmas was almost upon us and I was excited, I thought he wanted to take me out to show me off to his friends. Put on your best clothes and get a baby sitter he told me, we will be out until late. I got the children to bed early before the baby sitter's arrived, they were called Wendy and Jeff, they had just got engaged and I knew I could rely on them. They told us to have a good time and not to worry about the kids or coming home late, they would stop the night.

I was taken to a beautiful big house, opposite the police station. I had no idea Alan mixed with such affluent people. I was introduced to a woman called Doris, who mentioned to Alan that her husband was sick and couldn't get that night. She took me into a large room where the table was laden with food and drink. I was amazed, I had never seen so much food; she mentioned that the cigarettes were for anyone who wanted them. There were several couples scattered about drinking and talking. Doris handed me a drink, made her excuses and left saying she would see me in a little while; she needed to go to the bathroom. Doris had a brother John, who introduced himself and then went over to sit with a woman in the corner. I learned later she was called Jane Reed. Alan sat me down at a table and introduced me to a man named Clive. Alan told me that I would be safe with Clive. He was just going to see someone about some business. After a short while, I noticed that a lot of the couples had disappeared. I was determined to go and find Alan.

I learned during our conversation that Clive was a homosexual; no wonder Alan said I would be safe with him. Not wanting to appear rude, I wished him Happy Christmas and told him I was going to find my husband. As I stood up to leave, I dropped to the floor, my head spinning. I remembered a red carpet, going up two flights of stairs, and lots of beds, lots of noise and lots of people. I don't know to this day what happened. All I can remember is waking up on three steps outside it was six in the morning. I had a lousy head and I just wanted to go home. All Alan could do was stand and shout at me.

"You useless slag, you can't do anything right."
I came to the conclusion that the drinks were spiked or the cigarettes were dodgy. I asked Alan what had happened, he said he didn't know, I hadn't been with him. As I said, I don't know to this day what happened. Alan refused to say anything else and the subject was closed. We arrived home and Wendy asked if we'd had a good time. How can you tell someone that you don't remember anything that went on during the last twelve hours? So, I just said.

"OK."
We had two more friends in the village called Edith and Mick, and they asked us if we wanted to go to London with them to see a show. We agreed, and made up a foursome. Alan said he would drive us there; we could stop on the outskirts and then go in on the underground. We all left our kids with their grandparents during the three days we were away. We went to see Marion Ryan in a show at the Palladium. The following day we all went to see Madam Tusaud's Waxworks, then on to the Tower

of London, followed by some shopping. I was really enjoying myself; this was how it was supposed to be when you're married, and I really got on well with Edith and Mick.

When we got back home they asked us if we would be Godparents to their twins, we both said we would love to. Later, Alan remarked that Edith was a bit of all right, but I brushed his comment aside, convinced that it was him just being clever again. Over a period of time, they stopped visiting. I thought it was just me being sensitive, believing that something was wrong. It wasn't until later, I found out that Alan had suggested wife swapping to them, Edith had obviously thought I was in on it. To this day, she hasn't really forgiven me; she just wouldn't believe that I had no knowledge of it.

During this time I was regularly visiting fortune tellers and spiritualist, in my ignorance going against God [See duetoromy C 18]

4

By now I was getting a lot of work singing, and earning a lot of money. I was billed as Grimsby's Shirley Bassey. I was on top of the world as far as my singing went, but life with Alan wasn't great, I was seeing very little of my earnings, he said he needed it for the farm. It was really hard work at that time whilst we were getting the farm on its feet. We were killing and salting down pigs, then rushing home to get ready for my singing at night. I had started to drink a lot, I don't know why. Maybe it helped me cope with Alan a bit better, or maybe, I just liked it. One night I came home drunk and went into the shed for some coal, Alan had left a garden rake on the floor, I stood on it and it hit me full in the face, knocking me out for a few seconds. When I came round Alan said.

"Get the coal in, stop moaning, it's only a scratch."

It didn't seem like a scratch to me, I had a big fluid filled lump on my head for days after the accident. I'd wanted to take the children on holiday, but Alan was having none of it, he had remarked that it would stop him from enjoying it.

We had some of Alan's friends staying with us at the time, and it was to transpire later, that the woman had been having an affair with my husband, whilst all along, telling me she was my best friend; I had been gullible enough to believe her. (I realised later that this was the reason why Alan hadn't wanted the kids to go on holiday with us.) She mentioned that I didn't look very well, I thought oh! Not again. Alan would have been really angry if we had have been going on holiday that week. We were going with Val and Keith, and Val came around the evening before our departure, I'd had no time to pack I was frantic. I had to get the children ready to go to their Nana's. Alan, as usual was nowhere to be seen. He would come home expecting everything to be done. I told Val I had to go to the doctors for some medicine for a bladder problem; I also had a bad headache. So she said.

"OK. I will see you early in the morning, goodbye."

I knew I was getting worse, but I didn't say anything until the kids had gone to bed. I told to Alan that I wasn't feeling very well at all. He just dismissed me, saying as he went out of the door to the pub.

"I've spent a lot of money on this holiday, get some aspirin and clear off to bed, we are going on holiday in the morning so be ready."

I remember moaning and making a lot of noise with the pain. When he came home in the early hours of the morning, he said.

"For God's sake shut your mouth, I need some sleep, if you don't be quiet, I will put you to sleep."

The next morning I was unable to move. It must have been about 4.30am, because Alan was up milking the cows, I must have dozed off again, the next thing I remember was Kay pulling at my arm, saying.

"Get up Mummy."

I wanted to speak but the words just wouldn't come out, all I could do was groan. It must have been very frightening for Kay; she was only two years old and Peter was six months and I knew he would need feeding soon. I managed to get the words out.

"Go fetch Betty."

Kay just said.

"No."

The more I pleaded with her, the more she said.

"No".

The next thing I remember was being helped downstairs into a waiting ambulance. It was now mid-day and a feeling that I needed to pray for my kids, came over me.

The excruciating headaches, the trembling and my body racked with pain; I can remember having felt like this before. I knew in my heart I had meningitis again. I was taken to the hospital and put into a room on my own and immediately given a lumber puncture. [This is when they insert a needle into the spinal cord, to draw off fluid]. I knew nothing of what had happened for weeks afterwards, all I recall was thinking that I had died and was laid in a coffin. Finally I awoke and the nurse, who had been my constant companion, asked me how I felt. I still could not talk and the pains in my head were indescribable. My spine seemed to have a mind of its own, it would seem to lift and then drop down again, such a weird sensation. I could not move; I learnt that I had been laid three weeks without any movement at all. My head throbbed constantly; I was taking thirty pills a day, plus injections in my behind, I felt like a pin cushion. The injections were crystallised penicillin and procaine. However, the worst of all were the lumber punctures. I remember the first movement was the finger on my right hand and eventually the whole arm began to move

Gradually my body started to respond to treatment. I remember my physiotherapist getting very excited one day, it had taken three months before they were able to lift me out of bed, and this was for only one hour. I was sat in a darkened room because the light hurt my eyes. I was still isolated from anyone else in the hospital; the physiotherapist came in every morning to see if there was any improvement on the day before. It was a long haul getting better. I was not allowed any visitors because of the isolation ruling.

After about five weeks Brenda came to see me, I had been cut off from the outside world for so long. I didn't know how my kids were; I missed them so much. They let Brenda in wearing a mask and gown; it was so good to see her. However, she couldn't tell me anything about my children.

The tests went on for hours, to see if there was any damage to my kidneys or any other organs. After six months I could make it to the chair on my own. I was allowed out on the veranda for short spells, my kidneys were not working properly and I had to have a catheter attached all the time. After seven months I started to move a bit better; I was not allowed to go near a mirror for some reason, so I asked the nurse to get me one. I was shocked to see I had bald patches on my head; I was so disappointed because I had always taken great pride in my hair. This image staring back did not look like me at all. The meningitis left me with brain damage, and I couldn't manage to put sentences together very well, nor even tell the time.

After being in hospital for nine months, Alan came to see me. The doctor told us I could go home, but I would need constant care. I heard Alan say he didn't want me home; looking like a zombie and not able to talk, he didn't have time to look after me.

The hospital sister called Molly and she agreed to let me go there, together with the children. I knew it was going to be hard for Molly, after all she had her own children; I couldn't do much and I slept most of the day. All I could think about was the fact that Alan didn't want us home. Later it started to get too much for Molly. They sent for my mother to come and look after us, she didn't want to, but it was either that or I would have to go back into the hospital. Molly had done her best by us, was just too much for her.

We were taken back home but Mum was no good at looking after a family. She had failed her own and she liked her own life too much. She soon started to neglect us all. The social services arranged for a lady called Dot to come in every day, from 7am to 9pm; she was excellent, she would wash and dress me and then look after the children. She would take them out for walks while I slept, give them their tea and get them ready for bed, before going home. Carol, my sister-in-law helped where she could, and another friend Betsy would do my ironing. The first thing I attempted to do on my own was to set the table for tea. I just couldn't cope I knew what to do, but my body wouldn't respond to what I told it. I was such a mess, I couldn't get the words out that I wanted to say; my children must have been very confused by it all.

It was at this time that Alan lost all his pigs due to an electric wiring fault on the fence. Someone had made this for him on the cheap. It ended up costing him dear, it not only wiped out his entire stock, but he still owed money for his feed bill. By the time he had paid everyone, it left him virtually penniless. He started to blame me saying it was my fault; I had brought him nothing but bad luck since the day he married me. I told him I would go back to work, to help cut some of his losses, but I knew I wasn't really well enough. I went to see the doctor. He said there was no way I would be able to go back to work, nor even be thinking about it, I would only end up back in hospital. Peter was now two, and Kay was four, I ignored the doctor and went back to work, leaving my mother-in-law to look after the kids, she was sixty and it can't have been easy, but I was determined to show I wasn't as useless as Alan thought.

Alan was prescribed nerve pills for his depression, caused by the loss of his business. The doctor had told me to hide the tablets from him, only giving him the prescribed dose, with one extra if he needed it. But they didn't help much and he only continued to drink more. His temper was now worse than it had ever been. Everyone was a waste of space according to him, even the kids.

Dot who had being looking after us while I was poorly, couldn't believe it when I told her I was going back to work. She tried to dissuade me but I was determined to earn my keep. I will never forget that first morning, it was 7.30am. I met Carol at the door, because she had brought her daughter to be looked after as well. As we walked away from the house, I started to cry, I was leaving the children alone again, I hadn't been out of their sight since I'd come out of hospital, Peter had said.

"Don't go out Mum."

I was very slow at the sewing machine, but I thought I would speed up as the day went on. The whole day went badly from the beginning, by late afternoon I was feeling really ill. A voice inside me was saying go home Joan, but I ignored it and carried on with my work until five o'clock. I arrived home at five forty five, dead on my feet. Only to realise there was nobody home. I went to my mother-in-law's to pick the kids up, but her house was empty too.

As I was walking back home passed the petrol station, the lady came out and asked.

"Joan how is he?" I said.

"Who do you mean?"
She replied.

"You don't know what's happened do you? You had better come inside and I will tell you what's happened."
I knew it was serious by her voice.

"At about three this afternoon, I heard a child scream, I thought at first someone had got run over, so I went outside. When I got to the door your mother-in- law was shouting for me to get an ambulance. Your Son Peter was screaming and asking for you, as far as I could tell, his arms and face were scolded. He was rushed to hospital.

She was amazed that no one had let me know. Her husband offered to take me to the hospital, I was so shocked and exhausted I couldn't think straight. I was speechless in the car trying to imagine what had happened. We picked my mum up on the way, it was eight o'clock by the time we arrived at the hospital. We got to the ward, and I asked the nurse where Peter was.

"Oh! So you're the Mother are you? You should be ashamed of yourself, what were you doing to let this happen? Your Son is in a critical condition in intensive care. Where have you been? He needs you."

My mum put her straight telling her, he had not with me at the time and that he was with his other grandmother. The nurse apologised, and showed me where Peter was.

I stared into the room I was so shocked to see this frail little body attached to tubes and wires and in an oxygen tent. I didn't recognise him at all. He was all swollen and red raw with the burns. I said.

"That's not my Peter; you have made a mistake." The nurse said.

"You obviously haven't seen burns like this before, the swelling is from his kidneys, he has third degree burns to his arm and face, the arm is the worst because they are sure it has gone quite deep, they will know more in the morning."

His right arm was fastened to a splint, I went and sat down near him and held his tiny left hand. I sat and prayed for him all night; I just knew he would be fine. My own illness and tiredness forgotten, I just wanted Peter to be well again.

I stared at my baby son the next morning. He was all bandaged and swollen beyond recognition. His arm in the wooden splint was all torn and burnt, the wound stank but I didn't care, I just wanted to sit with him until he got well. I prayed to God that if he let Peter live, I would never go out to work again while the children were little. I didn't know then, but his trauma was to last two years, until peter was four.

It was a few days later that I found out what had happened to Peter, Alan's mother was boiling a cauldron of beetroot on the fire; Peter had climbed up onto a chair, and fallen, pulling the beetroot on

53

top of him, causing all these horrific burns. Over the next few months they had to do a lot of skin grafting to his arm, to do this they took good skin from his legs. But after three attempts and after gangrene had already set in, they decided to scrape it back to the bone and treat it with deep radium. All this time, his father hadn't been to see him once. The doctor asked me to sign for the treatment, as his father had refused to sign. Apparently, there was a risk of Peter not being able to have children of his own in later life. About a week after signing for the treatment, I wasn't feeling very well, so I went to see the doctor. He told me something I didn't really want to hear, that I was pregnant again.

John and Doris came to stay to help with the milking as well as looking after Kay. My time was taken up going to see Peter. I used to take Kay on odd occasions, she liked to visit, but she had to go to school, so much of the time I was on my own. I was feeling quite ill, being pregnant again. Once more I went to see the doctor. He was very angry, and said.

"What are you thinking of, getting pregnant again after all you   have been through of late, didn't you stop to think?"

I was so taken up with visiting Peter, I hadn't noticed that Doris and John had stopped coming. One day whilst on my way to see Peter, a woman in the village stopped me and said.

"Joan, didn't you know that Doris is pregnant and Alan is the Father?"

I called her a liar, but she told me she would prove it.

"You're a fool Joan, you walk around with blinkers on; John is divorcing her."

I went to see Peter as planned but left early. I was determined to find out the truth. I got on the bus for Barton; I had not seen Doris for three months. I arrived at her house, but when I knocked on the door nobody answered. I looked through the window, only to see Doris sneaking into the back room to hide. John, who had not left, came to the door and shouted for Doris to come out and face me. When she came out I could she was as far gone as me, at least six months. She didn't say a word just stood there and cried. John said.

"Now you know the truth, Alan is the father, she can stay here until she has had it, and then she can go. I am getting a divorce. Good luck with the baby Joan and I hope Peter is going to be alright, but if you take my advice, you will get rid of him."

He obviously meant Alan.

I can't remember getting home on the bus, I was so hurt, he had promised he wouldn't do this again, but this was worse than the last times, this time he had got someone pregnant. When I got home Mum was there, I remembered, I had said she could stay for a while, because she had just had an operation. I was devastated, what could I do, I was really trapped now Mum had arrived. I began to feel so alone; I started to visit Alice a friend down the road, just for someone to talk to. I was still visiting Peter at the hospital, getting Kay ready for school and looking after Mum, it was all very tiring. I just went onto automatic pilot and ploughed through everything

Mum asked me one day what was wrong. She didn't know anything, I hadn't told her about Alan and what he had done. However, she was very insistent that something was wrong. I broke down

55

and told her everything; she was so angry she didn't offer me any comfort, all she said was.

"You have Peter in hospital and you're pregnant again; you must be stupid or something."
I just stood there in total shock. When Alan came through the door and heard us shouting he asked.

"What the hell is going on in here?"
He looked at Mum and said.

"What the hell is wrong with you?"
At this Mum spun round on him and started to telling him what we knew about the other woman. But he ordered her out of the house saying.

"Mind your own bloody business."
I was still crying, but he never said another word. Mum got into taxi and went to Molly's.

My sister-in-law had seen Mum crying and on finding out what was wrong, she said to Alan.

"I will never speak to you again; you haven't looked after Joan at all, especially with all that she's been going through, how could you stand there as if you haven't done anything wrong?"
Alan just told her to shut up, and turned to me and said.

"I will be upstairs, shout me when teas ready, and don't be long." Carol said she would help me all she could, and then left.

Alan told me he loved Doris and would have divorced me a long time ago, if we hadn't had the kids. He said.

"We will make a fresh start and I will not see Doris again."
He sold the house and we moved to Killingholme, (to see if we could work things out). This seemed strange to me, as I was the victim in all this. I was shattered, Peter was due out of hospital; we were

soon to be moving, and all I was told by Alan was to put it all behind me.

The doctor told me there was a problem with the pregnancy, he thought I was having twins, we should put the off the move until after the birth. There was a setback with Peter; it would be another two months before he would be coming home; so we decided to wait.

I started with labour pains about the sixth of January, I was eventually taken into hospital four days later, and whilst undergoing examination the nurse confirmed there were two heartbeats. The pains got really strong and all I could think was; I am going to have these just like I had Peter. How wrong I was; I drifted in and out of consciousness for seven days. I was really well looked after by the nurses who were monitoring me constantly. In my stupor I remember hearing the words.

"That's one away, but no heartbeat."

I didn't panic because I was too drugged up, I really didn't care.

They took me back to the ward, one hour later John was born. He was very battered and bruised because they had to deliver him with forceps. I was allowed one quick look at him and then he was taken away to be cot nursed. The baby born before John; was stillborn; I didn't even ask whether it was a boy or a girl, I was so exhausted. The staff were very good, they kept referring to the baby as little Charlie and told me he was doing fine. The first time they brought John to me, I recalled that Doris would be having her baby about now. I started to muse while I was laid there and began thinking of all Alan had said; that he didn't love me, or even care about me. He hadn't loved me for a long time, if indeed he had ever loved me at all. I knew when I got home that I would have to start thinking about me, and what I was going to do now. I loved all three of my children, but I was utterly trapped; I was twenty-six but felt a hundred. I knew in my heart I would leave, but as to when I didn't have a clue.

After the birth, whilst the doctor was examining me, he found a growth on my womb. I was sent for a cancer test on my bowel. During the whole of my stay in hospital, Alan only came to see me once. After four weeks I went home with my new baby. I didn't say anything about the growth to anyone. I stopped having anything to do with Alan sexually and just went into denial.

Just after arriving home I was told that Peter would be coming home the next day; I was so excited to be having all my children together. I was still very ill after having John; I got a nasty infection in my kidneys. However, I managed to cope with all my "duties" as well as looking after the kids. I used to go to bed for a rest whenever I could.

During this time Alan took a job driving, and he used to be away all week, only coming home at weekends. It was at this time I began to have an affair with a neighbour called Walt. He was married to Alice and I used to go round and confide in them about what I was going through with Alan. It was after one of my visits that Walt asked me to go out with him one night; I thought it would be fun; not stopping to think of what this would do to Alice and their family. I was just thinking of me. It would give me a chance to get one over on Alan. My health had started to pick up a bit now, so Alan decided it was time to move to Killingholme.

Just before we moved, Alice asked me to go round. She said.

"Joan I know what Alan has done to you, but I also know what you have done to me."

I felt so ashamed; words just wouldn't form in my mouth, I said nothing in reply. She went on to say.

"Is this how you repay my friendship? Oh don't worry you aren't the first and I don't suppose you will be the last, but I thought better of you."

I pleaded with her to forgive me. She said.

"I will forgive you, but don't get in touch with me or Walt ever again."

Those parting words haunted me for months, and I swore I would never hurt anyone like this ever again. I told Dad that we were moving to Killingholme. He and Gran were pleased because they would be able to see more of the kids.

We got settled into the house, I got Kay into school and Peter into nursery. I still had to take Peter to hospital to have checks on the grafts every three weeks. I still didn't trust Alan. I knew he was still up to his old tricks. I just had an instinct that he was seeing someone else, but I had no idea who. So I decided to be brave and ask him outright, I needed to get things sorted in my head, after all I was getting like him. All the time he had asked me to swap I had refused, but now, I too had been out with someone else. I thought I had been getting my own back on Alan and teaching him a lesson.

When he came home that night I asked him if he was seeing someone else. I told him the truth and said I'd had two affairs. He got very angry and said he was not going out with anybody, saying.

"I thought we were going to try again."

It went very quiet for about ten minutes, and then he said. "I have a plan."

He said that if I would go wife swapping with him he would let me stay for the sake of the kids. But I flatly refused and told him I would rather leave than do such a thing. His answer to that was; that no one would touch me with a barge pole if I left him and that if I left, I wasn't having the kids. I didn't say anymore and told him I would think about it. I was frightened at the thought of not being able to have the kids. That night after I went to sleep I had a dream; I dreamed I had got a carving knife and had stabbed Alan repeatedly, until he was dead. In my dream I was taken to court and accused of murder. I was standing before the judge, who said I had been found guilty, and he sentenced me to be hung.

I woke up with a start, realising what I was capable of and what he had driven me to. I had to make plans to leave. I knew if I didn't, I would eventually kill him. I carried on with life as best I could, knowing that I was in a situation that only I could do something about, but for now, I had to carry on if only for the kids.

The new house was lovely, but I was worried about Peter, his arm wasn't healing properly where they had done the grafts. His face and leg had healed fine but he was far from well. I knew he was a fighter and he would win his battle in the end. Alan's brother Bill was getting married, and Peter was going to be a pageboy while Kay was to be a bridesmaid. I felt so proud when I saw them both. John was starting to fill out, and getting quite chubby, I too was feeling quite well. I used to go to

Gran's a lot during the day. She and Dad loved the kids.

I started to do oil painting, but life with Alan was becoming more unbearable. The crafty punches when no one was about, the snide remarks about my lack of interest in his sort of sex, and what he would like to do to me. He would threaten me when he came home at night saying that he would show me what real sex was like. I would lay awake all night too frightened to go to sleep. I was relieved when he came in drunk. I could put up with the verbal abuse, but I knew he wouldn't be able to do anything to me sexually. I used to hope he would come home drunk every night. My wishes came true because, most night's he did. I had a friend, who had a baby the same time as me, I used to confide in her a lot, but she moved away after suffering a rough time with her husband and she eventually divorced him.

One day I was really suffering badly with kidney pains, I was on a mild dose of morphine. I had been busy with the children but managed to get them to bed. Alan came in and said.

"Where's my bloody dinner?"

I told him it wouldn't be long, but that I didn't feel very well. He had just come in straight from the garage, and was covered in oil. He insisted he had his dinner right then and not later. I said.

"You can demand all you like, you will have to wait, and I will get it ready now."

He got angry and pulled all the pans out of the cupboard.

"There." He said. "I have helped you now get on with it; I want it when I come down."

61

He went upstairs, leaving oil everywhere, even on the ironing I had just finished. By the time he came downstairs again he was even angrier and asked.

"Where is the milk bottle I take to work?" I replied.

"It's in the sink waiting to be washed."

He took it out the sink and smashed it onto the path outside the door, shouting,

"You lazy slut you haven't done anything today."

He went back upstairs, got changed and went to the pub.

I just sat and cried, wondering how I was going to clean the mess up. I thought once again about getting away. We had some friends up the village called Keith and Kath, I thought of asking Keith to help me but how could I approach him without bringing the wrong kind of attention to us, because Kath had left him and it would look suspicious.

The next day John became ill, and I could not pacify him, he just kept on crying. I was dreading Alan coming home. He had worked a double shift and the last thing he would want was a crying child. I did the best I could, I managed to get the kids to bed about 8.O'clock, and I stayed up with John. About ten thirty I heard Alan come in, I ran downstairs to get his dinner for him. He just picked up the plate and threw it at the wall; he threw it so hard it went everywhere. John woke up and started to cry, I went to him and Alan shouted.

"Shut that little bastard up before I get up there, or I will."

I knew he wouldn't like John sleeping in our bed, but I thought it's the only way he will be quiet so I brought him into bed with me. Alan was still downstairs; I could hear him banging the cupboard doors. He shouted.

"Where's my bloody cake?" [Alan always had a cake after his evening meal].

"It's in the pantry." I shouted.

John was now burning up with fever. He cried even more; this woke the other two. I got out of bed to try and calm them down. Alan came running up the stairs pushing past me and dragging Peter out of bed, he said.

"The little sod's eaten my cake."

I started to laugh because I was frightened, I said.

"Inspector Jerrard and the case of the missing cake."

Peter was stood in a daze and stuttering said.

"I don't know about the cake."

I stood in front of Peter and told him to go back upstairs. Alan knocked me to the floor, I got up and took John upstairs and took them both into Peter's bedroom and shut the door. Alan kicked open the bedroom door and grabbed me by the throat he said.

"You cow, I am going to strangle you".

By this time John was screaming, so Alan let go of me and went for John. I got hold of John and said.

"You don't touch him, he's poorly and I am taking him to hospital."

Alan followed me out the door, and cool as you like asked the neighbour if they could look after the other two, while we went to hospital, just as if nothing happened. On the way there I was thinking I could not bring the kids up like this, I had to do something, even if it meant losing everything. I decided to show the hospital staff my bruises and the marks on John's body that Alan had inflicted in his temper. I gave John to the nurse and she told me he had a temperature of 104, the doctor gave him an injection. He asked if I was OK and I said.

"Yes thank you".

Alan then said to the doctor.

"I had to bring him in; I have been very worried about him."

It was 3.30am; the doctor said he would keep him in for observation that night and told us to ring later on that day.

We went home without saying a word to each other and went straight to bed. I later rang the hospital, and the doctor told me there was little wonder he had been screaming. He had chickenpox and the spots were all internal. He told us we could fetch him home, provided we kept him in. Two days later the other two were covered as well. I wasn't quite sure if this was a blessing in disguise, as Alan didn't stay in because he wouldn't or couldn't stand illness. He worked a double shift on a Saturday, and this was when I started to pack a few bits and pieces and hide them away from Alan. I had finally started to make plans to leave. I didn't have much of a plan but at least I had made some sort of a start. That day, all I did was tend the children and their spots, placing cooling flannels on their foreheads.

Once more I thought of Keith, so on Saturday after Alan went to work, I left the children with Val and told her I was going to the shops and wouldn't be long. As I got near to Keith's, he was just coming up the road on his way to work. I flagged him down. I didn't know really how to approach him, because he was a quite person and didn't bother much with anyone. He stopped and asked me what was wrong. I said.

"I need help but I don't want anybody else knowing about it."

He said.

"If you can get away about five O'clock, I will meet you after I leave work."

I told him that I would, but asked him not to tell anyone. I knew Alan wouldn't be home until ten, so when I got back home I asked Val if she wouldn't mind coming back later, so I could go to see Gran for half an hour. She said that she would, but not to be late. I gave the children their medicine and got them ready for bed, and told Val I wouldn't be late. I met Keith at the top of the lane; I explained to him how I needed to get away with the children. He said.

"I expected you to say this, so I have already asked my friends if you can go and stay there for a while."

He told me that he would take me the following Saturday. I said.

"But the kids won't be over their chickenpox by then."

He told me his friends June and Jerry knew about the kids being poorly, and that it didn't matter.

When it got to be Wednesday night, I tried to talk to Alan one last time, just to tell him how I felt, and to reassure myself that I was doing the right thing. I asked him why he didn't love me, and asked if he loved Jane Reed. He said.

"I love Doris, I told you that already, and I still do. I don't think I have ever loved you; you're useless."

I told him I would leave and take the kids, but he said.

"If you go it will be without them, anyway who would want you with three kids; they must have a screw loose, if you take the kids I would find you and take them back. When I have finished with you nobody will want you. You won't be worth looking at never mind fancying."

That remark made my mind up for me, I was going.

On the Saturday I was ready. I had packed three blankets and some clothes for the children. Alan had bought a new car and told me he didn't have any money. All I had was my family allowance book. When Alan went to work I went through his pockets, and found a hundred pounds, but I just put it back. I didn't want his money. I had ten pounds and thought that would keep us going for a while. Just before ten I had one last look around, before Keith picked us up. I didn't take anything, only what was in the case. I got Kay up first and put her on the back seat under a blanket, telling her we were going on holiday. Keith got Peter whilst I got John. I left Alan a simple note on the table saying.

"This is it, don't come looking for me. You can see the kids when I find somewhere else to live, meantime, don't try and find us, or I won't even contact you. Thanks for the good times, there were three that I can remember, and I have them with me."

I started to cry on the journey to June and Jerry's house, it was just after one o'clock in the morning; they lived in a village just outside Grimsby in a two-bed bungalow. June helped with the kids when we arrived, and together we got them off to sleep. Keith told me he would go home and come back the following week to let me know what was happening back home. All I did was cry all night, I had no idea what lay ahead, but I would go see Brenda once things settled down. June said we could stay until I had decided what to do. I slept on the settee. When I awoke in the morning, Kay was stood beside me, she said.

"You said we were going on holiday, you lied to us."

I told her we had left Dad because he had been bad and had found someone else.

"When we find somewhere to live you can go and see him".

The kids were still poorly with the chickenpox; John was the worst. I was unable to go out for a while. June and Jerry were both at work so we were on our own most of the day. I knew my name would be on the missing persons list by now, because Alan would not sit back and do nothing. I started to think of Kay's schooling and drawing my family allowance. This would draw attention to where we were. I also knew this was final and Alan and I would have to go see a solicitor about a divorce.

5

June looked after the kids whilst I went to see a lawyer; it was the first time in eleven years that I had spoken to a stranger about my marriage. I told him everything, the wife swapping parties, the beatings, and the mental cruelty. He was amazed when I told him he had taken all my money from singing. He advised me to go for a divorce on the grounds of mental and physical cruelty, unreasonable behaviour and adultery, he also told me to go for custody of the children. He said I had custody anyway because I had them with me, but we might as well make it legal.

I went back to June's house feeling good about myself; I felt I had won a round for the first time in my life. I really had to find somewhere to live; June was so good to us, but I knew I could not stay there for too long. I had to get the children back into the habit of going to school. I also needed some money to give to June for our keep. I knew deep down I was in for a tough fight with Alan, he would lie and cheat to get his own way.

I got Kay into school the following week; on her first day I went to meet her at home time. As we were walking home, Kay said.

"Mum, guess who I have seen today? Cindy and her mum."

I couldn't for the life of me think who Cindy was, let alone her mum, who Kay had said was called Maureen. Kay said she had told her to tell Daddy where we were living. I panicked because I had no idea who she was. I was to find out later, that Alan had been visiting her while her husband was away at sea and he had been taking Kay with him.

When I got home I explained to June what had happened. I now had to go and find somewhere, before Alan came looking for us. I got the newspaper and looked through the ads. I decided to go into Grimsby the next day to look around for a flat. I looked at numerous places, but couldn't find anywhere that would allow children. I had been out looking for seven hours. Keith was at June's when I got home, and he helped me to look through the paper again, he came across a caravan site in Scunthorpe. June made enquiries to see if there were any to let. She was told that there was a van, and I could move into it that night. I had no possessions to speak of so Brenda gave me some pots, pans and some food. I was determined to keep hold of the kids. Kay had started to ask to go back home since seeing Maureen. She was constantly saying.

"I want to go home to Daddy."

I should have been seeing the doctor at regular intervals, but these visits got pushed to one side. All I could think about was getting out, because I was sure he now knew where we were. I put the kids into Keith's car and said a big thank you to June and Jerry. They assured me that they wouldn't tell Alan where to find us. Off we went again, with only five pounds in my purse for the first weeks rent, and the food Brenda had given me.

When we arrived at the caravan site, we were taken to a small touring caravan. I asked the owner if this was all there was? He said.

"Take it or leave it."

I was so desperate; I took it. When we got inside it was filthy. Leaving us in the middle of this mess, we were to now call home; Keith left and said he would call during the week sometime. Peter and Kay helped me clean it the best way we could with what we had. Kay didn't have a lot of respect for me and said she wasn't stopping in this mucky hole. I was just pleased to get us somewhere and was determined I was going to clean it and make it home. I don't know why Kay was the way she was, maybe it was because I hadn't been there for her the way I should have, what with my illness and Peter being in hospital. She maybe felt safer with her dad. I think deep down, I feared that I would loose her to her dad. I kept trying to reassure her, telling her, one day we would have a nice new home but I knew she wasn't listening to what I as saying.

The next day we carried on cleaning, there was a stale smell and I couldn't figure out where it was coming from, we looked underneath the van and there was an old bath full of stagnant water; we managed to drag it out and empty it, the smell was awful. We worked hard all that day getting it fit for human habitation.

The following day, I went to social services to get food for John, and some clothes for Pete and Kay. I also managed to get Kay into school. Peter didn't have a pushchair and it was a long walk through the woods. Kay hated it and kept repeating that all she wanted to do was go home. I decided then, that I would not give up custody but agreed she could go on access visits. Alan had found out where we were, so I let both Kay and Peter go to see him for a visit, on the strict understanding that they were to be back by six. This became a regular thing but after every visit Kay got worse, saying she wanted to go home. Peter noticed how worried I was and one day said.

"Don't worry Mummy, I will look after you."

His arm had barely healed, but he would go outside to the tap and fetch water in a bucket. We also managed between us, to put a bit of wallpaper on the walls, with the help of some nail scissors and flour and water mix.

We were now coming towards winter and living below the poverty line, it was a real struggle. I told the landlord that I needed a bigger place to live. He said.

"I have got one, but the rent is five pounds a week, a pound more than what I was paying. I told him I would like to have a look and he agreed to show me around, it was a lot bigger, so I told him I would take it. Kay and I carried all our belongings to our new home. It took a lot of cleaning, but we managed, and it looked quite nice. Kay seemed to enjoy cleaning it out, and I started to hope she would forget about going back home to her dad.

I met a girl across the way, called Marlene, and she asked if I could look after her little girl and boy some days whilst she went out in the daytime, I agreed that I would. She told me she had to go see her boyfriend, who was in Hull prison. Marlene would give me food for looking after them, which was a great help. I wondered where she got all her money from, because she was on the social just like me. Eventually she told me. She was prostituting herself in the daytime. I asked her how she could do it, especially while he was in prison, she just said.

"What he didn't know, didn't hurt, anyway how else am I going to pay my way and feed the kid's?"

I started to look after them more often. She would go out all night and then pick the kids up the next morning. I was even doing her shopping, but the money she gave me helped with my kid's food and other little bits. Keith came to see me, However, he was only there ten minutes, and told me he had to go see someone, but wouldn't be long. He came back after midnight. I told him I wasn't going to put up with that, I'd had enough with Alan. I told him to go and not bother coming back. The next day when I told Marlene, she said I was well rid of him. I didn't find out until later, he'd been late back because he had been in bed with her.

Molly came to see me and brought Dad with her, he pleaded with me to go back to Alan, but I said I wasn't going to live the way him and Mum had done. He gave me ten pounds and said he wouldn't come and see me again in this place. A week later Molly brought Gran to see me, she cried but after I explained the situation, she understood, and said.

"Look after yourself."

I missed her so much after she left. The next day I had Marlene's children all day. She had been to the prison to see her boyfriend; it was six o'clock that night before she came home. Her Son had lost my door key, but Marlene said.

"Don't worry it will turn up."

Kay, Peter and I, searched all the van inside and out, but could not find it. Marlene then tried her key in my door and it fitted, she said she would lock my door when she went home, and told me to use the bolt on the back door until we could get another key cut. I was very unsettled that night.

After I finally got the kids to sleep; I sat up in bed and read a book, not daring to go to sleep myself. Suddenly the door opened and a man came in with a knife and two bottles of beer. He said I have brought you a drink, Marlene told me you needed company and cheering up. The kids thankfully, were asleep because it was quite late. I asked him how he had unlocked the door; he told me Marlene had lent him the key. I told him I didn't drink but he sat down on the bottom of the bed and said he would just stay awhile and chat. I asked him to please leave. By this time he had opened the beer and started to drink, I told him I didn't want my kids wakening, he said.

"Just do as I say and no-one will get hurt."

My ordeal was to last most of the night. After repeatedly raping me, he sat on the bed and started singing the song, Nobody's Child. He told me he was an orphan, and that nobody cared about him. Finally he left, saying he would come back again another day. I was just pleased to get him out of the van. I felt degraded, filthy and utterly repulsed by the whole experience; I didn't say anything to anyone, because he had threatened he would come back and hurt my children. Marlene came over later and told me she was really sorry; it was all her fault, because she had given him the key.

The next day Marlene asked me to go out with her to the bowling alley; saying she would get someone to look after the children. I told her I didn't want to go out, but she insisted, saying that it would do me good. I told her I didn't want anything to do with the way she lived. After assuring me that there would be no men, I agreed to go, but only for a couple of hours. I explained I wouldn't be able to drink because of the tablets I was on. She said.

"Well just have one drink you don't have to go mad".

The babysitter came and I left Kay watching the television with her.

Together with two shillings and sixpence of my left over money, plus two cigarettes; we walked from the caravan up into town to the bowling alley. There was a nightclub underneath called Tito's. It was a bitterly cold night, and it must have taken us an hour to get there. I was now beginning to wonder what the hell I was doing. On entering the club, we put our coats in the cloakroom. I told Marlene I would go and find us a table and said that all I wanted was a bitter lemon. She said.

"Oh! Come on, have something stronger." I said.

"No, that is all I want."

I found a table in the corner, and sat waiting for her to come. There weren't many people in as it was still early for a nightclub. Marlene brought my drink over, and just as she was about to sit down, four men came in, so Marlene went back to the bar and left me there with my drink. She kept waving for me to go over, but I just shook my head. She came over to me and said.

"Come on, we can have some fun with these four." I still said. "No."

She called me a miserable bitch, so I said.

"You go back to them, I will have my drink and go, and I'm worried about the kids anyway."

74

It never occurred to me I had no idea how to get home. I knew Marlene was annoyed, and she stayed at the bar with the four men. I was under no illusion as to what she meant by fun, but I was convinced she could manage to cope with them on her own.

Suddenly the place seemed to fill up from nowhere. I took a cigarette out of its packet, and felt quite embarrassed when I realised I didn't have a match. A young man from the next table noticed, and came over and gave me a light. We talked for a while and then he asked me if I wanted a drink. I told him to clear off; I wanted to be alone with my own company. I said.

"Anyway I'm going home."

He offered to take me home. I told him not to bother; I was twenty eight years old and had three children, hoping this would put him off. But he insisted, saying that he wasn't bothered about my age or the kids and he would still see me home. This made me feel safe; he would at least I hoped know how to get there. I finally agreed to let him take me home, I got my coat and told Marlene I was leaving and went to phone for a taxi.

Whilst we were waiting for the taxi we were chatting and exchanging names. He told me he was called George. Suddenly, during our chat he kissed me. It felt wonderful; it had been a long time since I had felt like this. We were so engrossed with each other that we never heard the taxi pull up until; he started to beep his horn at us. I couldn't help but think I had seen George before, it wasn't until much later I remembered; God had given me a vision of him a long time ago, when a friend of mine got killed on his motorbike. I also remembered God saying I wasn't to get married until I was twenty-nine. This made me realise what a big mistake my marriage to Alan had been. However, whatever mistakes I had made, I had three lovely children and I couldn't regret that.

I could not remember having been kissed like this before. We got into the taxi; the drive home didn't seem to take any time at all. When the taxi pulled up outside the caravan, George said goodnight, and asked if he could see me again. I asked him to come in for a coffee, he said.

"OK."

He paid the taxi driver and we went inside. He was still there the next morning; we had fallen asleep in each other's arms on the settee. I didn't ever want him to go. When the kids got up, I tried to explain who this strange man was. Peter was alright about it, but Kay was so angry saying she didn't want him there. George said he would go, and see me later, when I'd had a chance to talk to the kids, but I said.

"No stay."

I didn't want to loose him now I had found him.

I decided to go on the pill now that I was going out with George. I managed to get them cheap from a man on the campsite called Paul. He was one of those people who, if you wanted something he could get it cheap and no questions asked. I accepted the pills not knowing where they came from, but they seemed to work. I didn't care; I knew I wanted to spend the rest of my life with George.

George was with me for three days before I even asked him about himself; we were so rapped up in each other I hadn't given it a second thought. I asked him what he was going to do. He said he would like to move in with us, and would go home to get his clothes. He went home that night, but I was panicking, thinking, he wouldn't come back; he'll be like all the rest. My heart raced when he returned three hours later with his suitcase. It was enormous and I thought he must have lots of clothes and things, but when he opened it there was hardly anything in it. He assured me he was prepared to take on the kids as well as me, and we would be a proper family.

I asked George what he had said to his parents; he told me he only had a Mum at home and he had told her he would be stopping at a mate's house for a few days. I couldn't understand why he had told his mum a lie, but I thought he knows what he is doing and anyway, he was an answer to my prayers. Now I would settle down with George and be a proper family. That week was the best week of my life. Though George had a job he didn't go to work, he stayed home with me. In fact he didn't go to work for three weeks.

Saturday came and I knew Alan would be here to collect the kids. He pulled up outside and waited for Peter and Kay. George hid while they had gone, which seemed the right thing to do for the time being. When they came back later that day, Kay insisted she was going home to live with her Dad. I knew it would be futile to argue, so the following week when Alan came to collect them, I told him she could go, although he couldn't have custody and they still had to answer to me. This broke my heart, I felt like the woman in the story of Solomon cutting the baby in half. 1Kings chap3 verse 16 to 28

George decided to give up work for a while until we got things sorted a bit. So he rang the company he worked for and asked if they could sort out any money owed to him, and he would go pick it up later. When he said he would go and fetch his wages, I said I would like to go with him, he said.

"OK. Get Peter and John ready, but it's a long walk."

I told him I didn't mind it would do me good. I didn't tell him that the real reason I was going, was that I was worried he wouldn't come back. When we got back home, George just gave me his wage packet and said.

"Get what you need."

I was so taken aback; nobody had done this for me before. I hadn't seen Alan's wage packet empty, never mind one with something in it. We sorted the money, went and got some shopping and paid the rent. George had been with me for six weeks, when he said.

"I suppose I had better take you to meet my mum."

She still thought he was with his mate. I hadn't even given it a thought; I was just revelling in the love and comfort we had for each other.

I was petrified as we set off, but George kept assuring me that it would be OK. All the way there, I was thinking of what she was going to say, after all, I was nine years older than George [or as George always puts it, its only eight and a quarter years] and with three kids. When we arrived she was a bit taken aback, when George told her that he was going to live with me. She said.

"Well you've made your bed; you will have to lie in it, but you know there will always be a bed for you here, if things don't work out."

George assured us both things would work out. After meeting George's mum I felt a lot better. She used to buy us food and bits of things, because she knew we didn't have much. I was convinced that this was going to last. And we went back to the caravan.

Kay went that weekend, it broke my heart, but I knew it was best for all concerned. Over the next few weeks Alan seemed to know everything that went on at the caravan site. We were later to find out, that a man on the site had been watching us and reporting everything back to Alan. George was furious and threatened to go and beat him up. I persuaded him not to do anything and calmed him down. Alan had already got Maureen in my house, with all my things. All this time Kay knew and hadn't said a word. He had told the solicitor she was his housekeeper.

One day George said that he had something to tell me; I asked him what it was. He told me that six months earlier he had come out of prison. He went on to explain to me what had happened. He and one of his mate's called Melly Dawson had broken into a garage and stolen some chocolates and other things. They had got caught and he was sentenced to two years in borstal. He assured me, he wouldn't be going back in again, so I accepted it and told him to put it behind him and get on with his life.

I made an appointment to see a solicitor about getting a divorce. When I got to his office, I told him all about George, he sat me down and said.

"You had a watertight case for a divorce, why didn't you wait until after it was all over to move George in?"

He picked the papers up and threw them in the air and said.

"You have just thrown it all down the drain."

I didn't know what to think. He told me I would now lose the case, but he would still fight for full custody and maintenance for the kids. I went home and told George what the solicitor had said. He said.

"Stop worrying because I'm not, the sooner it's over, the better, as far as I am concerned."

George told me he was going up to Tito's to see his mates, to tell them what he was doing; he hadn't seen them since moving in with me. I was worried, and he could see it in my face, he assured me he wouldn't be long. Another incident that worried me was one night after George took me to his mum's. He told me he had to go somewhere to see someone. When he got back, I was shocked to see he was all dirty, with his face all marked and bruised. I asked what on earth he had been doing. He said.

"We are hard up and I remembered someone who owed me ten bob [50pence]."

Apparently the chap had refused to give it to him, so he beat him up and took it out his pocket. This bothered me because George was on licence, and could be sent back to jail if he caused any trouble.

One night there was a knock on the door, I went to answer it and a man was stood there asking to see me. George was behind the screen so I asked him in. He then asked if he could see George as well. He told me he was a private detective, whom Alan had hired. When George came out he asked if we had been sleeping together. George said sarcastically.

"No, we are just good friends, of course we have been sleeping together, there are only two bedrooms and the kids have one. I am not the lodger so you figure it out, if that's all you want to know, clear off and don't come back again."

When he had gone, George said.

"It's for the best; just get him off our backs, so we can get on with our lives."

During the next few weeks, I became really ill, I got horrendous headaches and I was still taking a lot of medication. George did what he could but he could not take the pain away. He said.

"We have to get out of this hellhole; it's too cold and damp."

It was now the middle of winter and we decided to apply for a council house, this place was no good, either for the kids or me. The mattresses were covered in mildew and the whole van was damp. I remember waking up one morning, and although the fire was still glowing in the fireplace, there was ice on the inside of the windows.

George was beginning to build up a good relationship with the boys. One Saturday when Alan was late picking them up as usual, the lads got fed up of waiting, so George took them out to play football. Alan arrived two hours late, and the boys were filthy, I panicked and said.

"I will have to clean them up." George said.

"No, they can go as they are; he should have been on time."

Alan didn't like it but George said.

"Take them as they are or not at all."

He decided to take them, but on their return, John was sitting in the back of the car saying.

"Never mind Pete, we will soon be home with Mum and George.

I rang Molly and asked if she would push the application for a house through at Immingham. She told me she would go on Monday. The days seemed to drag waiting for an answer. We had no money, George didn't have a job and I didn't want him to get one. I thought if he got a job, he would start going out with his mates again and would leave, so we plodded on and waited. I started to rely on George to help me with the children; I'd had to do everything, mostly on my own up until that point. I remember one day we didn't have much to eat, [Alan was refusing to pay maintenance] so we went for a walk, and lying in the road was a leek, someone must have dropped it out of their shopping bag. Peter picked it up and took it home for tea; the problem was; what to have with it. George told me he was going out and would not be long. He came back later with some potatoes, and two big wood pigeons, I didn't ask where they came form, we just enjoyed the meal.

Alan continued to pick the boys up on Saturdays. One day when John came home, I could tell something was wrong. I asked him what was bothering him and he started to cry saying.

"George is not my dad."

How do you explain to a two year old that the man you live with; is not his dad? I asked Peter what had been said he told me Alan had been saying things in the car on the way home. I went to the phone and rang Alan and said.

"If you don't stop upsetting the boys, I will stop you from seeing them."

The following week Molly came with my gran, she was very upset at our demise, but I assured her we wouldn't be here much longer. Molly said, she thought we should hear something by next week, regarding a house in Immingham.

Winter was well on us now, and Molly had invited us to their house for Christmas. So we packed the few little toys we had managed to buy the boys and Molly picked us up. We didn't have a lot of money, but Molly and her husband George took us to the local club on Christmas Eve, and we really enjoyed it. We all spent Christmas Day with Molly and her family. I had arranged for Alan to pick the boys up on Boxing Day. When he arrived he came in and started acting big, telling George how he was going to get the divorce, and how he would take George for every penny he had. George was quick with his reply however, and shut him up by saying.

"That's OK. You won't get that much, you will have to get it from the social, because that's where we get ours from."

Alan soon decided it was time to go.

It was time to go back to the caravan, but we were grateful to Molly for what she had done. The next few days were agonising, we didn't have any means of heating the water, so George asked his brother if we could go to his house once a week for a bath. He told us we could, but he used to frighten John. When ever we went anywhere after that, he would say.

"We are not going to Bill's are we, not today? Even if we were going, we would tell him.

"No." just to keep him quiet.

George's mum was good to us, she helped us whenever she could, but she lived quite a long walk away. His younger sister Sharon used to come down with her friend to see me; I liked Sharon, I could talk to her, even though she was only fifteen.

The following week, Molly came and said.

"I have some good news, Immingham Council have given you a house, and they want you to go view it, to see if you want it."

George and I both said.

"We don't need to see it, anywhere is better than this dump; when are we able to move in?"

She told us she would go see the council and get the keys as soon as possible. I knew it would be a wrench for George to leave his family, but he said it would be OK. He could come over on the train and visit them. We got very excited over the next few days. We didn't say anything to anyone; the less people that knew, the better at this stage.

Molly said she would pick us up the next day, so told us to be ready. There wasn't a lot to do, basically, it was what we were wearing, plus a few bits, even the telly wasn't ours it was rented, George had modified it, so we could use the same coin every time. Molly came early the next day as promised and we loaded the car. She said.

"You had better take a mattress you will need something to lie on."

It actually belonged to the van, but we thought he has had enough out of us we didn't owe him anything. It was six o'clock in the morning, and there was no one about. They must have had a shock when they realised we had gone.

6

We arrived at Immingham, where, Molly drove us to a new housing estate and to Langley Walk, our new home. It felt good just to be surrounded by bricks and mortar and have real windows, instead of that dreary van. Molly had managed to get us two old chairs, a bit of carpet and an old telly, that when switched on, had the sound and a picture that was all shades of green, an old gas cooker, the oven didn't work, in fact when George went to light it the first time, he nearly blew the place up. We had some curtains for the front window, which we put up in a fashion and closed them so the neighbours couldn't see in, but we were happy. Alan had refused to give me anything out of the house, not even my own personal things. George said.

"Don't bother he can stick it."

We soon managed to get a few things together. Molly introduced George to a friend called Ron, who said he might be able to get George a job on a construction site. He gave him the name of the site manager. George went down the next day and they told him he could start in a week. When he came home and told me he'd got the job, my first thought was, what am I going to do, we hadn't been apart in six months. However, I realised we had to start to make something of our lives.

We made the most of the rest of that week together. On the Monday morning George went to work as arranged and I went with Peter to get him into school. While I was out I met a girl I knew from schooldays, and she asked me if I still sewed. I said.

"Yes."

She informed me they were looking for machinist in the local factory, so I went and got the job. I knew I had to find someone to look after John. Molly said she would have him initially, and later Ron said his wife would take him for me. So that was it, we were both working and the kids were a lot happier.

The divorce papers finally came through, naming George as co-respondent, but we didn't care, we were free of Alan. At long last, we could do what we wanted to do now. We made friends with the young couple who lived next door, they were Irish and their names were Ed and Kay, we got on really well with them. Kay had a friend called Eileen. She was telling me her baby had just died in hospital and that her husband didn't seem to care, it sounded a bit like Alan. Eileen was later to play quite a large part in our lives.

Things were beginning to get better, we started to fill the house with furniture, and George went on twelve-hour shifts, it was two weeks on nights followed by two weeks on days. Everything really started to look up. When George was on nights we used to pass each other in the morning, he was coming home and I was going to work, but it didn't matter, we loved each other and knew this is how it had to be. We were to live in the house for just eighteen months.

We decided it was time to venture out and buy a place of our own. We didn't have the deposit because we had spent a lot of money getting things together for the house. Kay and her husband offered to lend us the fifty pounds we needed for a

86

deposit, and we purchased a house in Battery Street, three doors from Molly's. By the time we moved into our new home, George's job was coming to a close; the contract was nearing its end. However, it wasn't long before he managed to get another one. He went to work for a scaffolding company, the contracting job had paid a lot of money, but this turned out to be just as good.

We got settled into our new home, both with new jobs. I was working in the local corner shop. After about three weeks, I found out, that there were a lot of people around us doing bed and breakfast. So when George came home that night I suggested that we should have a go at doing it. He said.

"OK."

We worked out we could feed six people for the money that two would be paying, and what's more, we could get them all into the front bedroom. This bedroom was large enough for three sets of bunk beds, six bedside cupboards and two wardrobes. After a few weeks, it dawned on us that all the lodgers used to go home for weekends. This enabled us to let the room to Swedish students who came over on the ferry. We were well off at this time, compared to many other people.

The court case finally came up at Lincoln Court. It was the most demoralising thing I had ever gone through. I lost custody of Kay, I was fined £50 by social security, and they took my family allowance book away from me for six months. I was awarded maintenance of two shillings and sixpence a week for the two boys.

One day I was taken home from work, I had suffered a miscarriage. I was to be in bed for three weeks whilst George looked after me. A little while later, I was still feeling very unwell and went to the doctors, after he had examined me he said.

"Congratulations, you are still pregnant."

I found out that I had been expecting twins. I rushed home to tell George, we were both over the moon. The time carrying the baby seemed to rush by. Eventually, came the time to go into the maternity home for the delivery. However, there were complications; despite the fact that I had only carried my baby for seven months, it was unable to get down into the birth canal. They had to take me down to theatre and manoeuvre the baby into place. One doctor said the baby was already dead. Then after a great struggle our baby daughter Sharon, was born. She only weighed three and half pounds and wasn't very well, but after two weeks we were allowed to take her home. She had only gained one and half ounces, but they said she would be OK. It was a huge struggle; she would not take her feed, and she was looking worse by the day. It was during this time that we let all the lodgers go, apart from one; he stayed on as he was such help to us. He would run us about in his car.

During this time my sister in-law Pam was arranging our wedding for us at the registry office in Scunthorpe. George's mum had agreed to do the sandwiches at her house; I was able to buy a short white laced dress. I borrowed a coat from my next door neighbour. We got a lift to Scunthorpe with my sister Molly; she had brought one of her friend's to be a witness

We were home within three hour's with a marriage certificate. No pictures because we could not afford them.Peter and John were excited and disappointed, excited we had got married disappointed because they could not be pageboys. We arrived home to wash nappies and get the kid's to bed

During the first three weeks of being home from the maternity home, we had the doctor out to Sharon several times. One doctor said she was a wee bad-un, and we should put her in the attic to cry. One particular time though, was different, this time she was cold and grey, and she was loosing a lot of bodily fluids. I was really worried so George called the doctor. He said he would come out in the morning, but I knew in my heart she needed attention straight away. George rang for an ambulance and told them it was an emergency. They arrived within five minutes; the ambulance men gave her oxygen, and looked up at us and said.

"It will be touch and go."

Sharon made a little whimper; it was the first sound she had made for several hours.

On arrival at the hospital she was rushed straight into intensive care. After being ushered into another room we were frantic, wondering what was happening. About two hours later a nurse came and told us they were still battling, and asked if we would like to have her Christened, just in case anything happened, we both agreed. The doctor came to see us some while later and told us Sharon had meningitis, a collapsed lung, and a heart murmur, but she was a fighter and was fighting for her life. He advised us to go home, where we would be more use than sat in the hospital. He would inform us if there were any changes. We sat holding hands for hours trying to give each other moral support.

We had left my sister in charge of the boys, but we found them wandering the streets when we got back. So we simply picked them up and took them home. There was a message pushed in the door from the doctor when we got there, telling us he had called but there had been no-one at home. George rang the surgery and asked to speak to the doctor. He thanked him for his concern but stressed that, if he had come out last night, as he should have done, things wouldn't be anywhere near as bad as they now were.

Sharon was in hospital for a whole year, during which time I was taken ill again. I went to the doctors, and he again told me I was pregnant.

"You cannot go on like this." He said.

"You have too much on, to be carrying another baby; I think you should have an abortion."

I said I wouldn't think of it, so he told me to go home and get some rest. I went home to Peter and John. I was crying and Peter said.

"Mum I can help? I have ten pence you can have." I said.

"Thank you so much love, but it will take more than money."

When George came home, I told him the news. I didn't really know what he was thinking; he didn't look as pleased as he had when Sharon was on the way. I told him I was alright but the doctor had told me to rest. George was on night shift, and the following morning I was feeling really ill, so he brought the bed down into the front room, so I didn't have to go upstairs. He was going backwards and forwards to the hospital to visit Sharon. The ensuing few months was very hard; I wasn't very well at all. John, our one and only lodger said he would take us through to the maternity home. It was a good job he'd stayed on, because it was quite a way to the hospital in Grimsby.

It was around this time that two young girls came looking for a room; they were called Hazel and June. Like me, June was pregnant; she told me she couldn't go home because her father would kill her. She had got pregnant to a married man. Feeling sorry for her, I took them in. I let them have the back room. June's baby was due around the same time as mine, and we helped each other out a lot. Hazel only stopped three weeks but June stayed. We managed to convince her to go and tell her parents. She agreed she would, so we allowed Pete and John to go with her to Barnsley and stay the night. Her parents were so pleased she had gone home, and she promised them she would go back again soon. When she got back, George helped her to sort her benefits out and she stayed with us until after the birth. She only came back to see us once after having of her little girl. I really missed her; she had been a good friend. I was never to see her again.

I told the specialist that I wouldn't have an abortion; it was against my principles. I knew I would cope, even though George had started suffering with bad nerves. I think the years of being a "yes" woman and the trauma I'd suffered had taken its toll; and I had finally said.

"No".

George was with me in the hospital when I went into labour. I had a traumatic time having Neil, and almost lost him. In the end I had to have part of my womb taken away. I knew this would be my last baby.

The day I came home with Neil, George went to see Sharon. When he arrived back home, he walked in through the door and said.
"I have a surprise for you."
He had Sharon tucked inside his coat, they had informed him at the hospital that she could go home. So he brought her on the bus. She was thirteen months old.

Our lodger John finally told us he had to go back home; which was a blow as George was, once again out of work. His nerves seemed to be going from bad to worse. He finally agreed to go see the doctor and talk about what was bothering him. He told the doctor about an incident that had happened to him when he was eleven. Apparently a group of teenagers had seized him, and tried to sexually assault him. There were six of them aged between eighteen and twenty years old. They hadn't succeeded but he was still tormented by the whole experience. The doctor was very sympathetic and put him on a drug called Triptazol, which he said would help to calm him down. They were quite a strong sedative; I had to keep waking him up to give him his next tablet. I was beginning to wonder what was coming next.

Peter and John really loved the babies. Then John became ill, his face was swollen and he had a temperature. He said.
"Mum I don't feel very well."
It turned out he had mumps. He was very poorly and to cap it all just as he started to get well; I began to exhibit the same symptoms; which was all

I needed on top of everything else, it was such a struggle. Peter was a little angel though. He would run back and forth to the shops, and never complain. George did his best to help, but by now he was worse and had a breakdown. The doctor said he was paranoid. He was on so many tablets; I was waking him up to take his next dose and when he was awake he was unmanageable, I remember he once told me to get out. I was so afraid because I was seeing the same symptoms in George as had seen in Uncle Frank. All I could do was to go out and sit with a friend. I never said anything to anyone about the way George was. I turned to God for help.

The Lord has given us a spirit of a sound mind [2Tim 1v7

When he was up and about a bit, he would go out and tell the neighbours that I was keeping him drugged up, and was generally treating him badly. Then the neighbours would be knocking on my door, telling me what a bad woman I was. When he wasn't in bed or out roaming the streets, he would just lie on the settee facing the wall, and wouldn't speak to anyone. He would have the light on all night; he was so terrified. I was at my wits end, not knowing what to do, there was no money coming in, and we were getting behind with the mortgage. I started to sell the furniture to raise money for food. One day we didn't have a thing to eat, the kids were hungry and we didn't have any gas either, (we had a meter that took shillings to get the gas.)

They say God works in mysterious ways. There was a knock on the door, and I went to see who was there. A lady stood there, I looked down and on the doorstep was a large box. She brought it in and said.

"Joan you need this for you and your family, there is also something for your gas meter."

George was in bed; she asked how he was and left. When we opened the box it was full of food and on the top was a ten-pound note. At first I thought the doctor's wife had sent it, but when I went to thank him, he told me it wasn't from them. I know that God had intervened that day and supplied our needs. I knew He had heard my prayers; this was to be one of the first miracles I was to experience.

We used to have a lodger called Podger Bill. George hated him, and the other lodgers didn't like him either. So he moved out and found fresh lodgings elsewhere in the village. One day however, he came round and said he wanted to know where he could get a new place to stay. I told him Jane Sayers would take him in. He asked where she lived and I gave him directions, but Peter offered to show him, I said.

"No you are not going."

Bill assured me he would bring him straight back. After twenty minutes I was becoming worried. I went around to Jane's, but she told me she hadn't seen anyone. I went to the police fearing all sorts had happened to him. He eventually arrived back four hours later, with a police escort. The police talked to Peter but when they asked what had happened. All he would tell them was that he had been to Cleethorpes with Bill. I don't know to this day what really went on, and Peter has never told me.

There didn't seem to be any improvement with George at all, so I got the doctor to come again. He was brilliant with him and suggested that he go and look for another job. George told me he would go to Scunthorpe to try and get a job on the steelworks. His Mum said he could stay with her during the week, and come home at weekends. While George was away the debt collectors started to come. When I couldn't manage to hide from them any longer, I arranged to give them two shillings a week whenever I could. I was trying to keep hold of the house but I knew deep down that if I didn't go to George's Mum's in Scunthorpe, our marriage would be over.

I told George what I was going to do, and he said he would ask his Mum if we could live there. She told us it was O.K. We managed to sell the house to the council, but at a loss. I collected up the few bits and pieces that we had left, and loaded them onto the local coal lorry, the driver had agreed to take us to Scunthorpe.

We arrived at George's mum's house, and put everything onto the front lawn, it must have looked a sight. She gave us the front bedroom as well as the downstairs room at the front. I don't think she realised what she had agreed to take on, with all our furniture, bunk beds, four children and a dog. It was a bit cramped, but it's the best we had at the time, George's brother Trevor was still at home, but kept himself to himself, we were so happy we could make a fresh start.

Things were not easy at George's mums, she would moan about the kids crying at night saying she had to be at work, and they were keeping them awake. One night, George had to fasten Sharon into her bunk with her reins usually used in her pushchair just to stop her getting out of bed. About an hour later I went up to see if they were OK, to my horror Sharon was hanging on the side of the bunk, she had all but hanged herself with those reins. We had to stay with Mum for eighteen months. I contacted Social Services in the hope that they would find us a house. George had a sister called Pam she would bring her children on Saturdays and leave them with me, whilst she went to meet her fancy man.

Mum worked Saturday mornings and on Saturday afternoon, it was clean-up time. The little ones weren't allowed out of the room until she had finished, and even then they were frightened to put our feet on the floors. She used to put newspapers down to walk on.

We finally received news that we could have a council house in Ashby, (a suburb of Scunthorpe); we were overjoyed and couldn't wait to move. The house was lovely but the décor was atrocious. The previous tenants had painted each bedroom door a different colour, but it didn't take us long to get it straight. I can remember thinking at the time that things were on the up again.

George's sister Sharon started to come round more regularly, while George and Colin (her husband) used to go to the pub for a pint. We had only been in the house for six months when George got made redundant from his job on the steelworks. He and Colin went looking for work; they walked to Killingholme and back, but there was to be no luck that day. However, he finally got a job with a piling company, the money was good and it was a long contract. We were finally getting good wages, and that Christmas I was able to get Peter and John some decent clothes for school, as well as new clothes for Neil and Sharon. I also treated Kay to a lovely musical jewellery box; the kids got real toys, the first for a long time. We even got them a bike each.

George had a nephew called Stuart; he was Bill's son, George's brother. He had been fostered out when he was young, along with his sisters. He was looking for somewhere to live, so we agreed to take him in, it turned out to be a disaster. He was accident prone he couldn't touch anything without breaking or damaging it.

George was going out drinking more and more, which didn't worry me unduly at the time because he was with either Colin; Stuart or sometimes Albert, an Irishman who lived across the road. His wife was called Pat and they had six children; we became quite friendly with them, and used to go to the club with them. I also started singing in the clubs again; we went to Lincoln, Boston and all around that area.

My gran, foster dad, and my foster brother, all died within the space of a few months. I missed them all so desperately. My foster brother was only twenty-nine, he suffered from Hodgkin's disease, but thankfully he had become a Christian before he died. I didn't understood how one became a Christian, and what it really meant to be saved at that time. It was during this period of my life that I felt I needed something more to cling on to, and although I was warned not to buy it, I bought an ouija board, thinking I could gain some comfort from it. We started having séances in the house, and some of the neighbours would come too. One night while we were having a séance the word Beelzebub came up and I said what does that mean, So George looked in the dictionary and found out it was the lord of the flies the devil, Then it struck me how wrong it was George would say it wasn't right and asked me to get rid of it. I didn't realise at the time just how subtle the Devil can be; you believe you are communicating with your lost relatives; but all the time you are weaving a tangled web of evil. I was later to find out how Satan deceives us and eventually possesses us. I started having bad dreams at night, about murders and all manner of evil things. I was beginning to think that this couldn't be of God, not a loving God, even the children were upset, especially John. Even the neighbours who started to come began having problems in their homes.

Things started to go dreadfully wrong with our relationship; as well as the rest of our home life. I was fool enough to take in a sixteen year-old girl called Linda from next door. One night George had been to the pub; and came back with this young girl, he had been with her most of the night. He told me he loved her; I didn't know what to do, so I told him to leave. He wouldn't go and kept saying he wanted to stay with me. I eventually spoke to the girl's Mother, she told me that the reason she had kicked her out of the house, was because she'd said she had slept with George. I didn't know what to do; it looked like I was heading for another divorce. I also found out there had been other occasions when George had been fooling around with other women. One was a married lady across the road. George was outside the house with her one night, and I refused to let him in. What a nightmare this was turning out to be.

One day I got a strong feeling inside, which I now know was the Holy Spirit speaking to my heart, saying forgive him, for he knows not what he is doing. In that moment I knew what the meaning of the crucifixion was all about. There was no way I could let go of another marriage.

Once again George had a nervous breakdown; he even said he would admit himself to a mental institution. Something seemed to be telling me to get out of the house and get rid of that ouija board. There were lots of things happening around me, things moving by themselves, things getting broken for no reason, even telling George to kill himself. One day he threw himself down from the top the stairs, and then ran into the kitchen and hid behind the cooker. Neil and Sharon were badly affected by all of this; they would do all sorts of things like, stripping off all the wallpaper and pulling the electrical fittings off the wall. Neil even sat out on the windowsill. One wrong move and he could have fallen fourteen feet onto the concrete. All the time I was thinking we needed to escape this house, not realising that no matter what we did the possession would go along with us.

George's sister came one day and said she felt sorry for me, she put her arms around me and hugged me. She said.

"I don't want you to be hurt, I love you Joan; you are more like family to me then any of my own family."

This felt really good to me; I had a vision of Jesus and he told me I had to forgive, because George didn't know what he was doing. Most the time I was repeating The Lord's Prayer and The Church of England catechism. I believe in God the father almighty, maker of heaven and earth, and Jesus Christ our Lord. His only Son born of the Virgin Mary, suffered under Pontius Pilate. Was crucified dead and buried, He descended into hell and on the third day he rose again and ascended into heaven. It just seemed to come over me first The Lord's Prayer and then the catechism. Then I would be saying get thee behind me Satan. I warned the children, and told them to pray. Everyone thought I had gone mad.

I went to see the local Church of England vicar, because I thought he would be able to help. After explaining what had been happening and I telling him that if he came over to the house he would be able to do something. He told me that I had given him faith. However, he did come to the house and pray.

Things had started to become really desperate. George was getting worse, and we were all sleeping in the same bedroom, because we were so frightened. I knew we had to get rid of that board; but it held a strange fascination that kept drawing us back to it. George had said all along that he didn't like it. So at last we decided to burn it; you would have thought there wouldn't be anything to it, after all it was only hardboard. We underestimated the powers it had. George lit a fire and put it on, but it took an age to burn. I now believe; that because of our dabbling with the board, Satan had gained control over our lives. I didn't realise it at the time, but the reason it wouldn't burn, was because the signs on the board were witchcraft signs and they belonged to the Devil.

Kay had been coming on and off to see us, but we had tried to hide things from her. One day she came and I knew there was something wrong. When I asked her what she was doing and how she had got here, she told me she had run away from home; she had borrowed money for her train fare, and asked if she could stay. She told me her dad and Maureen had been arguing, and Maureen had hit her. About an hour later, her dad, Maureen and Aunt Pauline arrived. We all sat and talked and it was agreed she could go stay at her aunt Pauline's. She would finish school and decide then what she wanted to do.

I felt the only way out from all this mess was to just leave the house as it was. I got in touch with Eileen at Immingham. She said we could go stay with her, until we found somewhere else to live. I knew that all I could do for George was pray. Peter said he hated George for what he had done, but I asked him not to, and assured him that things would be OK. We took Linda with us, as I didn't know who George would choose, all I knew was; I had to love Linda. Even though I didn't know whether George would still want me, because she was convinced he would choose her; although I knew I would win in the end. I just couldn't face the thought of another divorce. We just walked out leaving everything except the clothes we stood up in and the kid's bikes, and off we went to Immingham.

We had been at Eileen's for about three weeks. George had been going back regularly to Scunthorpe to pay the rent. Every-time he went I thought I wouldn't see him again but he always came back. Our problems however, were another matter they were not to be left behind in Scunthorpe they had just come with us. Eileen kept telling to me to send Linda away, but I knew eventually she would go of her own accord. When that day eventually arrived, she told me she would be going home to her Mother's, that she was pleased she was going and how she hated me for being so nice to her, she couldn't stand it anymore.

George got a job at a factory in Immingham, and I had to look after my children as well as Eileen's three, because she had decided to go to Ireland. She told me they were going for a few days but it turned out to be five weeks.

It was during this time there was a knock on the door, and when I answered it there was a small dark haired gentleman stood there. He said.

"Are you Joan?" I told him I was. He said.

"The Lord has sent me because you need help." I was stunned but also relieved, that someone seemed to understand our problems, so I asked him in. He said his name was Pastor Grossmith, with him was a lady called Doris, his deaconess. He told me he could help us with our problems if we would go to his church, which was on an estate in Grimsby, about ten miles away. George was at work and I said I would have a word with him, and let the pastor know. He told me he would come back the following day. George arrived home from work and I told him what had happened, he agreed to go to the church to see what it was all about. I knew then that church alone would not be enough, I needed more, and I was going to find it.

That week, everything that could go wrong, did go wrong. The kids ran amok in the house; George decided that he wouldn't go to church after all. Eileen didn't come back from Ireland. So I too cancelled going that Sunday, promising I would go the following Sunday. The pastor said he understood, and would continue to pray for us.

We managed to get through to Grimsby the following week, and finally made it to church. The people were very friendly, and I felt such warmth when I walked in. We sat through the service, and I realised that I had a problem. George didn't say anything, apart from commenting that the service was nice. Over the next few days, Pastor Grossmith counselled me with regard to my demonic possession. He asked if I would like him to pray for me. I told him that I would and he assured me he would go away to fast and pray for a day. He said that my possession would only leave by fasting and prayer.

Ten days later I went to the church with the pastor and Doris. They sat me down and started to cast out the evil spirits from within me. It was horrible, whilst they were praying, I saw hundreds of demons leaving me, and they had just heads without bodies. The pastor just kept pleading the blood of Jesus over me. He continually commanded them to come out, in the name of Jesus. I was there for about two hours. Finally the pastor said it is over, I felt a great relief. I found out the next day, that the estate where the church was, had had a terrible attack from the devil that night, especially the pastor and his family. I fasted for three weeks afterwards; I asked to be filled with the love and the saving grace of Jesus, I renounced the devil and all his works. I started to sing in tongues, it was awesome to me. I was soon to be deflated though when a man came up to me saying that this was of the devil, I was so hurt. I asked The Lord to take this away from me and I have not sung in tongues since. I just thanked God for His love, joy and peace.

That night I woke up to an attack from the forces of evil. I was confronted by what seemed like hundreds of demons trying to get me to go back to spiritualism. I had to cling on to the promises of Jesus, and He showed me a vision of Heaven and Hell, and the great void between, I knew I was safely in His arms. I gained much comfort from the Psalms, and Proverbs. I was singing in church, and giving my testimony to everyone who would listen. I had Jesus stickers all over, I wanted everyone to know, that I loved JESUS. As the weeks went on, we were going to church regularly, and the counselling sessions went on. George and the children finally gave their lives to Jesus, and we all went through the waters of baptism together.

One weekend an evangelist was coming to the church that had a healing ministry. I already knew The Lord could heal by His mighty power, due to the healings I had already received, both mentally and physically. So I asked Eileen if she would like to go, I knew she suffered a great deal from arthritis. I was thrilled when she agreed to come. During the service the preacher asked if there was anyone who needed a healing from God. Eileen went forward and told about her suffering, the man laid hands on her and she was miraculously healed. I couldn't understand why she wouldn't come back to church after that. I found out later that a lot of people take there healings but don't go back to thank Him. It's like the account in the bible where Jesus healed the ten lepers, but only one went back to thank him.

7

The Council finally gave us a house, just across the road from Eileen's. George said he would arrange to have our furniture brought from Scunthorpe. I asked Geoff, a friend of mine if he could fetch it for us, and he agreed. George and Pete walked to Scunthorpe, to start packing all the things. When they arrived they found Linda and her friend had been living in our house ever since we left. He told her to leave because we were moving the furniture out, and we had to hand the keys back to the council. They got everything they could into boxes, and moved everything from upstairs to downstairs; they were there most of the night. But by the time they came home everything was already to move, so I rang Geoff, who said he could do it in two days time.

We were on the move again. Two days later, I got the keys and George went to get the furniture. The house was filthy, but it was our new home. It didn't take long to scrub it out and it was clean by the time George arrived with our worldly goods. After we got settled, I suggested George should take driving lessons. We bought a car from Molly and Ron who took George for his first lesson. He promised he would take him regularly between his normal lessons. I can remember him going for his first test, which he failed, he was very angry and declared he could have pushed the examiner through the air vent in the car. He eventually passed at his third attempt.

George went to look for a job, but he was rather fed up when he came home. One of the questions had been.

"Have you been in prison?"

Because he was supposed to tell the truth, now that he was going to church, he confessed that he had been in prison and didn't get the job. I tried to tell him that it wasn't meant to be, but I don't think he believed me. The very next day, he went out and got a better job with more money. I knew then that God had better things for us, in the not too distant future. We were going to church on Sunday mornings in Grimsby; and to our local Methodists in the afternoon.

George was now earning good money but the hours were long and I didn't see much of him, he would go to work on Monday, come home at night for an hour, and then go back all night.

Not long after George had given his heart to The Lord and we had all been through the waters of baptism, we were going to house meetings, as well as church, we also started to teach in Sunday school. One day I invited a lady called Thelma round to see the change in George, and tell her what The Lord had done. We arranged for her to come after George got home from work. To my horror he arrived home drunk. He said The Lord had told him he could have a drink with his workmates. I bundled him into the bath to try to sober him up. How I prayed that both The Lord and Thelma would understand.

The next few weeks were pretty normal, that is, until one night George said that The Lord had told him to buy a bus, convert it and go to Australia. A few weeks previously we'd had some girls staying with us that were part of a choir from Australia. We shared with them about what The Lord had laid on our hearts. They said they would pray for us and if it happened, they would meet us when we arrived in Sydney. We promised we would stay in touch with them whilst we were on the journey. After the girls went home, we went to our usual house-group prayer meeting, where we were given a word of prophecy. Which was that we would come to a place where we would be surrounded by water and would be unable to go backwards or forwards and it would be here where we would make a big decision? We were puzzled as to what it meant, but we never forgot it.

I asked God to make me all things to all men; that I might help to save some. We started to tell people what God had done for us; some listened, whilst others scoffed. George's mother said to the rest of the family.

"Our George has got religion."

Some people listened and started to go to church and surrendered their lives to Christ, not George's mum though. I felt sorry for George, he had gone to see her expecting something good to come out of it, but she would not listen, she just said.

"It's alright for you but don't pester me with it."

One of the people we spoke to was an ex-prostitute named Val. She came round and knocked on my door one day and said.

"My friend Thelma said you are the God woman, I want to get saved, show me how."

I explained to her what salvation was about, and she knelt down on my kitchen floor and gave her heart to Christ. Both she and Thelma started to go to the church with us after this.

We stared to have prayer meetings in our house; this led to our first encounter with the super Christians. You know the ones I mean, never had to struggle at all, everything handed to them on a plate. One such a man came to our house for a meeting, and someone asked where the toilet was. He sarcastically said.

"It's down at the bottom of the yard in a bucket."
I thought as I looked at George's face, that he was going to tell everyone to leave, and probably knock this man out. But God clearly had His hand on the whole situation, because George just sat there and ignored him, calmly directing the person up the stairs to the toilet [Praise the Lord]. We also got two students from Germany through the student exchange system. We all had trouble with the language barrier, but we gave them bibles and they took them back home with them. The children really loved Sunday school.

The prostitutes used to call me the God women, and they used to bring there sewing to me. One woman called Rita came regularly she was "The Madam". She used to tell me I could earn money if I went on the game. I ignored her comments and just carried on testifying what God had done. It was hard trying to convince them that they could pray for themselves, but they always came to me to tell me their troubles, but I didn't mind it gave me more opportunities to witness to them. We took an old man under our wing, called John. He had the nickname soft-shoe Sammy, because he always wore plimsolls. He was a sly old fox but God loved him nevertheless. I used to do his washing and give him his meals, and other bits and bobs when we could. He had a drink problem, and his own family would have nothing to do with him, in fact they had totally disowned him.

We found out that there was a bus for sale in a village about ten miles away. I knew God wanted me to give up our home again. George made arrangements to go and see the bus. Andy, a friend from church agreed to take us; it was a fifty-three seat single decker. We had a good look around it and asked the man how much he wanted for it. He told us he wanted eight hundred pounds, which is a lot when you don't have anything. George said he would buy it, but he would have to raise the money. The man selling it asked us what we wanted it for as he had a lot of people interested, including Barry Sheen. Who it seemed, wanted it to transport his motorbikes. George told him we were going to use it to go to Australia. So the man agreed to let us have it, but he would only hold it for six weeks. We really had to trust God for the money; after all, we were far from well off, in fact we were struggling to make ends meet as it was, but we were tithing, and that's all God asks.

The next few weeks were a bit hectic; everyone seemed to come with his or her problems. We were also praying as to where the money was going to come from for the bus, but we knew it was right, so we left that with The Lord. I didn't get on with Andy as well as I should have done, and one day The Lord told us that Andy would be going with us. I dreaded the thought, but The Lord assured me that this was right, I spoke to George about it, and we decided that if it was The Lord's will, it would come about.

Then The Lord put us in touch with a lady called Ruby, she was a dwarf and deformed, but nonetheless we felt strongly about her coming too. As I have previously stated, The Lord works in mysterious ways. Ruby was to be God's instrument in getting the bus. When we mentioned to her what The Lord had laid on our hearts, she offered to provide the money for the bus. I used to sing in church, and one night after I had finished singing, Ruby came up to the front and testified as to how The Lord had healed her of depression whilst I was singing. Isn't He wonderful?

It was two days before our six weeks deadline regarding the bus. On the night that George went to collect it, he seemed a bit hesitant. I hadn't realised at the time, but he had only driven a mini, and had only passed his test three weeks earlier. However, we went for the bus and the man told us he had started it up. He showed George the instruments and the mechanics of it. We paid him the money and George sat behind the wheel, the man must have noticed how nervous he was. So he offered to drive it back to Immingham for us and said George could stand beside him and notice of what he did. The next morning there was a knock on the door, the person stood there said.

"You can't leave that bus parked there its not allowed."

Well, however much George was worried about driving it; now was not the time to fluster, it was the time to overcome. He got in and started it up and it was as if he had been driving all his life. The verse that comes to mind is; I can do all things through Christ who strengthens me. He certainly did it for

George that day, and still continues today. He parked it in a park behind the café.

During his spare time he altered the inside to make it suitable for travelling and living in. He took all the seats out except the front four, built bunk beds for Andy, Peter, John and Neil, partitioned these off and put in a bunk for Ruby and Sharon. We had a bed settee in another compartment and at the rear of the bus there was a kitchen and toilet. We had a tin bath, a dolly tub and posher. He used every available space for storage of tinned and dried foods needed for the journey.

George however, was still going to work all the time he was fixing up the bus. Finally it was finished, now we had to pray about the next move. We felt The Lord was telling us to go live in the bus straight away. I asked a friend of ours called Rose if she knew anywhere we could site it. She told us of an old airfield near East Halton. We decided that was where we would go. Andy and Ruby didn't come with us straight away, Peter didn't want to leave the house; it was a real wrench to leave. We eventually got in the bus and set off. We parked up on the first night and it was good, we felt free, nobody to bug us. We were in the bus going from place to place. George was still working to bring in some income. A local businessman offered us a place to park on his property until it was time to leave. He provided us with running water, and electricity. He even offered us his credit card to use when we went. However, we prayed and decided that we would not be fully trusting God if we accepted his offer, so we explained our position to him and he said he understood.

I felt so sorry for George, because he would have to walk across the fields to get to work, sometimes at midnight. Then we met an old man who owned a Jaguar car and he told George he could borrow it for work, which was a great help, but it was old and sometimes it wouldn't start, During our time at the site George decided to do some alterations to the bus, we got the owner of the land to make us an extra tank for the coolant water, which we connected to the original. George also managed to get some spare wheels from a local scrap yard, and six spare cylinder head gaskets. Ruby came to join us, but not Andy. I was busy making curtains, and also decorated each bunk. We were about to spend our first winter in the bus, so George made double-glazing for each window, we bought ten twenty-five gallon water butts for fresh water also ten calor gas bottles for heat and cooking. I painted oil pictures on the outside of the bus [This, we were to find out later happened to be a "God" incident, because in Turkey and Iran they paint pictures on all their large vehicles]. The inside was a real credit to George, as he had never undertaken anything like this before; He had even made space to live in during the day, and it converted to our bedroom at night.

Peter was now sixteen and had got his first job at a local factory, he bought a motorbike to get to work; everything appeared ready to me. I asked George if we were going but he told me he was waiting for a special tool to come then it would be time. He didn't know how long it would take but he knew that he wouldn't set off without it. A friend of ours from church also brought George a few tools that he thought might be useful, should anything go wrong.

We had a friend called Ada and she had family in Scotland. She helped me pack all the food under the bunks, sugar, tea, dried eggs, peas and meats etc., George said she could come with us, and when it was time to set off, we would go to Scotland first. She was so excited and started to ask when we were going. We knew though that it would be in God's timing, not our own. That time wasn't long coming; the postman arrived with a parcel, with George's awaited delivery. He had already worked his last day at work, and we got everything loaded up. Andy had sold his car and was now with us. Peter had left his job and sold his motorbike, which almost broke his heart, he had worked so hard to get it. We waited for Ada to arrive and then said our goodbyes to the friends we had made. We went over a weighbridge to get a record of the weight, ten and half tonnes fully loaded.

Before we set off, we had to call in at George's works to pick up his last pay packet. All his workmates had all put together and bought him a pair of binoculars. The kids thought they were wonderful, they all wanted to look through them at the same time. We were finally on our way, out of Immingham and heading for Scotland. We had contacted Ada's daughter and she had arranged for us to stay on a farm while we were up there. It was a long hard drive for George, as this was the first time he had driven it any distance, not to mention actually finding the place.

We finally arrived in Kirkintilloch just north of Glasgow. We parked the bus outside Ada's daughter's house and went to meet the farmer. When George saw where he had to drive to park the bus, he was a bit worried as to how he would get it up the winding road. We later discovered that Brenda, Ada's daughter was having problems with her husband. He was a prison officer at Barlinnie prison, and had recently told Brenda that he was gay. Brenda was a Christian and loved The Lord. She asked George one day if she could come with us. He told me that he could get another bunk in where Sharon was. So we suggested that she should pray about it and we would pray too. However, she couldn't make her up mind. I don't think it was meant to be, but George had been willing to take her and that's all God asks of us, to be willing.

George, together with prayer and a lot of determination managed to get the bus along that winding road. Once we had settled down a bit, we encountered our first problem, the carpet down in the bus was black and we didn't know why. George got under the bus and discovered the exhaust pipes had totally collapsed, hence the black soot all over the carpet. Willie, the farmer said he would take George around to see if he could get some new parts. They were three days going from place to place before they managed to collect everything together that was needed. It took George nearly all day to repair the exhaust, by the time he had finish, he had just about renewed the whole lot. Willie then asked George if he could dig some drains for him, because he needed somewhere for the sludge to run when he swilled out the cowsheds. George told him that it would be hard work, but he and Peter got stuck in. It took the two of them two whole days and a lot of sweat, but they finally got them in. Willie could not thank them enough.

We visited a few church's around the area, and told them what we were doing and what God had done for us. George went to see Willie's dad in hospital and we all prayed that God would touch him. Within two days he was home, Praise the Lord. Ruby told us she had a desire to be baptized, so George did it in Willie's bath. We were also confronted by our first encounter of a devil-possessed child. The child had been adopted, and the parents didn't know much about the child's real parents. All they knew was that they couldn't do anything with her. When we first met the little girl we discerned the evil in her. In fact the possession was so great, it made me physically sick, I was so embarrassed, but the child was miraculously delivered. I was threatened by the devil then I had a vision of God's royal robes in the house. I knew I had God on my side and couldn't lose. The parents were grateful for our prayers and they are ongoing Christians.

It was almost time for us to leave; we had to get Ada home. George had arranged to meet a friend called John, who was going to help George put an extra fuel tank on the bus. We said our goodbyes and set off back to Grimsby. When we eventually arrived, George and John fitted the extra fuel tank. This would enable us to carry a hundred gallons of fuel. It took them quite a long time to do it, so we stayed with his wife Hilary. They were finally satisfied that it would work alright and picked us up about four hours later, and we set off for London. We had to go to London to arrange insurance and visit various embassies, to get visas, and any information we could for our travels. By this time our story had hit the newspapers. The headlines were; Family give up everything to travel by road for God.

Our few days in London were a bit hectic; we parked in several locations during our stay. While George, Andy and Pete went to find the different embassies, we visited a Baptist church where they prayed for us to get things sorted out quickly, they made us very welcome. We finally got the insurance and some info on how to travel across places like Iran and Afghanistan. George got an itinerary put together, and booked the ferry at Dover. We were on our way.

8

It was quite daunting, when we first went on the ferry, as well as the realisation that this was what God wanted us to do, none of us had been anywhere or done anything like this before. Prior to meeting me, George had never been out of Scunthorpe. The ferry trip was awful. It was quite rough and I was sea sick, we were pleased to get to France, even though we didn't know what this trip had in store for us. We put it into God's hands and left the details to Him. We met a lot of young kids in a red double Decker bus; they told us they were going on the Australia road. We managed to get a lot of information from them and explained to them what we were doing. They thought a Jesus bus was a great idea, and said they would think of us on our travels and maybe we would meet up somewhere along the way. We never did see them again.

We travelled through France stopping only to rest at night. The route we took reminded us of England, with a lot of farming country. We crossed over the border and into Germany we met some young people in Kalsrhue, and explained to them what we were doing. They said they would come back later, with some friends, we prayed about this and we felt The Lord wanted us to move on before they came back, so we packed everything up and left. We didn't understand why, but God did. We found out later, that these gangs would operate in this way and then rob whatever they could. We crossed a busy street and George headed up to the border crossing, which he thought was Austria but then realising that the checkpoint was for East Germany, he decided to do a swift u-turn, and go in search of the proper border crossing.

After a lot of prayer, we eventually arrived at the border crossing with Austria. It is beautiful with its lakes and mountain scenery; unfortunately it was here that we had our second major trial with the bus, one of the airbrake cylinders had gone. George decided to drive slowly to the next village. Whilst travelling along the road we saw in the sky, a double rainbow, which is a promise from God. When we arrived, a man came out to greet us and we tried to explain what had happened. He told us it was now too late in the day, and to worry in the morning about what to do. We settled down for the night and the following morning he told us to follow his daughter and she would show us the way to a garage that would fix our bus. We just couldn't take in how God was blessing us, bearing in mind the bus was already twenty years old and we were in a foreign country. The garage had the right part on the shelf, and had us up and running within the hour.

We travelled along the road to a small place called Kufstein it was beautiful. I managed to get some washing done there. George boiled the water and filled the dolly tub; I put the washing in, got the dolly legs and carried on with it whilst the men went for a swim. The next day it was off again through the Felbertaun tunnel into northern Italy where we had some lunch, then off again into Yugoslavia. What a day, breakfast, dinner and tea, all in different countries.

Yugoslavia is a very poor country, particularly where we went. We felt sorry for the people who were digging amongst the rubbish for scraps of food. I left a bible with a man in the car park. We travelled through Yugoslavia for over two days and then crossed over into Greece. We spent two weeks in Greece, and in a place called Kavalla, we met Fred from Birmingham, who had moved out here to live, and he had his own private beach. It was whilst he was on the beach that George got bitten by something on his foot he was in agony. The only thing I could think of to do was to get the sting out, so I sucked on it until at last it came out. We found out later it was a rockfish, which has a big spine on its back. Whilst we were at Fred's house, which was beautiful, we met his neighbour's, whose daughter was suffering with meningitis. We asked her parents if we could pray for her but she was a bit frightened because she was Greek orthodox, she was worried what the priest would say. But we convinced her we served the same God. George and I prayed for her and we saw the relief come over her as God touched her. I also made Fred's wife a dress during the time we were there; she was really pleased with it.

George was talking to some continental lorry drivers and they asked where he was heading. They advised him to park up wherever he saw lorry's parked. It was finally time to leave Greece. We said our goodbyes and headed off for the Turkish border. We found Turkey to be a poor country, and the people who worked the farms looked poor and bedraggled.

Just after we arrived in Turkey, George noticed something wrong with the cooling system. So we pulled up into a lay-by and he went underneath the side of the bus. He found a leak near one of the cylinder heads. The problem was it was right in between the two heads. He decided he would have to change both head gaskets, which would prove a bit of a challenge, seeing as he hadn't had any experience with anything like that before. George and Pete were under the bus for nearly four hours in 105 degrees heat but they managed to do the job. George then had a couple of hours sleep before setting of again. I did wonder at this point why Andy hadn't said he would drive; after all he had come along as co-driver.

We went into a local shop for some milk, but all they had was goat's milk and yoghurt (when I say yoghurt, it wasn't the fruity type it was the real stuff, it was horrible and tasted sour, we couldn't understand how they could eat it). That night I had a vision about a lot of dead babies piled up in a heap. There was one baby who was still alive however, and I rescued it form the mess. I was puzzled as to what it meant but The Lord was to reveal the answer years later (which I will explain later in the book).

We arrived in Ankara, and we stayed for two days because we had to get visas to gain entry into Iran. The Iranians proved to be a bit difficult. We felt they were going to hinder us, but who can stand in the way of The Lords will? We finally got our visas for Iran, but they insisted that we only stayed in the country for seven days. We set off for the border, it was getting quite late in the day. George said we needed to find somewhere to park up for the night, but there didn't seem to be anywhere suitable to stay. So George carried on driving; it was now getting quite dark and up ahead we saw a light in the distance. When we reached it we realised they were Turkish soldiers, so we thought we would be safe. One of them told us in broken English we would have to stay there for the night due to some trouble at the border and we were not allowed any further.

We pulled into the centre of the village, and got the children settled down for the night. We then heard a lot of noise coming form the front of the bus. Ruby said.

"The soldiers are fighting with George and Andy.
I picked up my bible and headed for the front. Ruby then said.

"Don't go they will start on you."
However, I ignored her and carried on. When I got to the front there were three soldiers and they were asking for cigarettes and whisky. They were armed with machine guns. I instantly heard God tell me what to do, so I waved my bible at them and said.

"We don't have cigarettes or whisky, we are Christians and my babies are trying to sleep."
It was as if The Lord had just picked them up and got them off the bus. We never heard another sound, and when we awoke in the morning they were gone.

We arrived at the Turkey/Iranian border. This turned out to be quite an experience, the border crossing was like a large chateau, and we all had to pile onto the Turkish side to go through customs. All except for George, who had to drive the bus across? We had a few problems from the start because when we went over to the Iranian side, the custom officials started questioning Pete and John about who they were. Because they had dark features, they thought they were "wanted" Iranians. I managed to convince them of who they were and told them that my husband was on the other side with the passports. I caught a glimpse of George through the door and pointed to him saying,

"There he is."

One of the officers asked Sharon if that was her daddy, she said.

"No".

I couldn't believe it, but we finally got it sorted and we were on our way into Iran.

There were pictures everywhere, of Ayatollah Khomeini at that time. They were trying to get the Shah to leave the country. We found out after we left Iran, that he had been exiled. It was a fearful place; we didn't leave each other's side for very long. We finally arrived in Tehran, the capital and found a safe compound to park in. We had to get information on India and Burma; as this was the way we had planned to go. We also needed visas to go through Afghanistan. We had to sign a carnie de passage for Afghanistan. This was a document to say we wouldn't sell the bus; we also had to get extra photographs for them. We found someone to take us to a photographer, but when he saw Ruby he refused to take her picture, saying that she was cursed of God. We told him that we loved her and God loved her too. Ruby started to cry and told us that she would return home. We wouldn't hear of it and insisted that she had the photos done. We managed to get everything sorted for the next leg of our journey. George was looking tired, it was hard work and I was massaging his back and shoulders with olive oil to relieve his aches and pains. We got as much info as possible, Burma looked as if it was impossible but we decided we had to try.

One day, we all went into the swimming pool at a holiday camp. John saw a young child in distress, he jumped in and pulled her out of the pool and we took her back to her parents. After we had finished swimming we went back to the bus. The girl's parent's came to thank us for what John had done. I'm sure they would have taken us back home with them if they could. The father was a Muslim and owned his own oilfield and they were there on holiday. They stayed and had tea with us in the bus. We talked about Jesus, and what he was doing in our lives. They invited us to go to their house in Abbadan (an oil rich region). But George had to decline this offer because we had a long way to go and we only had three more days left in Iran. Anyway, we said.

"God bless you."

They understood we were unable to stay any longer and they thanked us once again and left.

The next day we were walking around the compound and we came across a Portuguese lady and her husband, he was an African. They were living in a small room with there two children. The young lady was in tears as she showed us where they were living. We gave them some blankets and food. They had been wealthy business people and had been thrown out of Africa by Idi Amin's regime. They had lost everything and they were now refugees waiting to go to Portugal. We told them we would be praying that there wait to get back home would be swift, and that their papers would be sorted out quickly. We assured them we would write once we were settled, and they gave us a contact address in Portugal.

There were also two English teachers, who told us they were travelling around on pushbikes. They had been all over and said they were also going to Afghanistan. Two days later it was time to leave, we travelled for sixteen hours until we were within distance of the Afghan border. We had been warned that Afghanistan was very strict at customs. We were not prepared though for what was awaiting us. Apart from the sun being blistering hot (135f) in the shade, we literally had to take everything that wasn't fastened down, out of the bus. Their customs officers came out in boiler suits and carrying a toolbox. They went through the bus with a fine toothcomb, looking for drugs. They even spent considerable time under the bus, dipping the fuel tanks to see if there were false tanks inside, checking the cooling system etc., Then I had to put all the clothes and food back, they had gone through everything.

We were finally cleared at customs and made our way into Afghanistan. It's a harsh country, rough and rugged and very hot and sticky. It was a hard drive for George all we could see in front of us was a long straight road that seemed to go on forever. Going through the first major city, we were aware of the strong Russian presence. We also encountered our first real sandstorm; George had to pull up by the side of the road. When the storm finally passed the bus looked as if it had been painted brown.

We finally arrived in Kandahar and pulled into a hotel park; they gave us permission to park in their parking lot. By now it was getting dark and George and the boys decided to go swimming in the pool. George dived in to what he thought was nice clean water, only to discover it was full of frogs and all sorts of other creeping things. Needless to say he didn't stay in there very long; he was out quicker than he went in.

The following day instead of us moving on, George decided to go to the embassy and find out about getting into India through the Khyber Pass. This was to prove difficult to go through as well as to get into Burma the route was definitely closed. We asked The Lord what we should do. George said he thought we should go south into Pakistan, over what the locals called Kojak Pass (real name Chemin Pass). When we eventually arrived at the pass, a man on a motorcycle said he would go on in front. George said he couldn't understand why God had told him to come this way, it looked impossible. However, we knew without doubt that it was God's leading, so with nothing but our faith intact we set off from a thousand feet above sea level all the way up to eight thousand feet. We got so far up and then we came to a halt, the bus would not go around the bend. There was a sheer wall to the left, rising straight up to about two hundred feet, on the right a sheer drop of about three thousand feet, the road was approximately nine feet wide. George got out of the bus to take a look. He decided that in order to get around the bend, he would have to take one of the side panels off, to allow enough extra room. We sat and prayed and Neil said.

"Mum if we go over the side, we will go to heaven and will God send a taxi with GOD1 on it?"

This lifted our spirits.

That night Neil sat and drew a picture.

We managed to put a huge dent in the panel, which was big enough to allow us to get around the

126

bend and we carried on up the mountain. We realised how much God was in this Journey because of the extra cooling tank he had us put on board. We finally arrived at the top where there was one lone border guard. I don't think he knew what to think. Here was this forty-foot bus coming out of nowhere; he asked us where we were going? He told us no one had ever brought anything this big up the pass before. We explained where we were heading, and he handed us all a big piece of cucumber, it was really sweet and juicy. George didn't usually like cucumber, but after he tasted it he actually asked for more.

We set off down the other side of the mountain, and when we got to the bottom we hit another obstacle. The road had been washed away and the water was running directly across our path, it stretched for about two hundred yards. This must have tested George's trust in God, there were three arches and we were unable to see which one the road went under. George drove very gingerly toward the three arches, and decided to go through the left hand side one. Isn't God wonderful, praise His name, He guided George through the water and kept the bus on the road. The scriptures say He will guide you and keep you, if you put your trust in Him. When we finally got to the other side of the water there was an Indian man, he took his turban off and saluted George for getting us through safely. We knew it would have been very dangerous without God on our side.

9

We finally arrived at the checkpoint into Pakistan, at a frontier village called Spin Boldok. When we parked up, the kids in the village were peering through the windows, wanting to have a look at this big bus that had come over the mountains. Peter was quite indignant, and said they were rude for squashing there faces against the windows. There turned out to be a bit of a problem, our exit visa for Afghanistan was for Herat not Kandahar, but we managed to explain what had happened. After what seemed an age we were finally allowed into Pakistan. George started to reverse the bus out of the compound, one of the border guard's insisted on directing him. He told Peter to get back on the bus and he would do it. Bad mistake! He backed us straight into a post and shattered the whole of the back window. George didn't even think about stopping to repair it, or indeed what to repair it with. He just decided that we had to get to the next town, which was called Quetta. It was a rough ride with the back window missing but thankfully it wasn't raining, or at least it wasn't at that moment anyway.

We looked over to our left and we could see the rain on the mountains. I would just like to take a moment to explain about the rain in this part of Pakistan. When you see rain on the mountains you know there is trouble coming. Because within a short time, we realised that all that rain had to go somewhere and we were right in its path. Another lake to cross, George said how weird it felt driving forward, whilst the water was running across your path. Once again, The Lord held us fast and we made it safely through. We then realised the consequences of not having a window in the back, when I looked the whole of the back end of the bus was caked in wet mud. It was in the toilet, the kitchen and all over the clothes I had just washed, it was awful. Everything was absolutely soaked and it wasn't just common all garden mud, it was thick red mud.

We finally made it to Quetta. After we parked up we had to start cleaning all the mud out from the backend of the bus. It looked an impossible task with the limited resources we had, but we managed to get it clean. We pulled up in a hotel yard; George had to decide what to do about the window. He decided that putting new glass in would not be possible, so he decided to fit some hardboard into the hole, it took him a while but he made a good job of it. When he had finished, I painted the outside with waterproof paint and we made it watertight.

We watched some Pakistani women doing their washing it looked quite funny, even compared to me using the dolly tub and posher. They were washing in the small stream and then banging it on the rocks, the children were quite amused by it. It was while we were in the hotel park that we got our first visitor, he was a policeman and he told us he was a "very, very," important person. He also knew somehow that we were Christians and told us to be extra careful; we were not allowed to talk about Jesus. They are quite comical in Pakistan, if they have any kind of authority; they think they are very important. Anyway, we talked to him for a while and told him what we were doing. He told us there were some nuns on a mission compound and we would be better off there. We thought it was for his benefit, so he would be able to keep his eye on us. We set off for the mission compound and found a place to park. By now it was late and we needed to get some rest, we decided we go and meet the nuns in the morning.

The following morning we got up and went to explore the compound. When we finally found the mission house there was no one at home, apart from a novice called Grace. She told us to call back at about two o'clock, when the other nuns would be back. As she suggested, we returned later and met the rest of the nuns. We got to know about Quetta, what to do and what not to do. We shared with them our plans, and they told us we wouldn't be going anywhere for a few days at least. We had hoped to go into India as soon as possible, in order to catch the ferry to Australia. However, we hadn't realised that this was the monsoon season; Quetta was completely cut off from the rest of Pakistan. Once again, we sought The Lord, asking Him what we should do. It was during this time of prayer that we realised the prophecy was coming to pass, exactly as it was told. We would come to a place where we would be surrounded by water; it seemed to us that this was the place. What would be the decision we would have to make?

During the next few days we discovered that nuns were having problems reaching the poor people, especially in remote areas. We then realised that, The Lord wanted us to let the nuns have our bus to use as a mobile hospital; it was perfect for their needs even down to the bunks George had fitted. We invited the nuns to come and look around the bus. When we told them of what The Lord's had instructed us to do, they were amazed. The nuns were of the Franciscan order and were quite free, very charismatic and open. The head nun told us she would inform Rome of what had happened. Two days later we had a visitor. A Mother Superior had come all the way from Rome, just as she put it, to meet this family all the way from England, who God had used to deliver a bus to the sisters. She had told us they had been praying for three years for something like this to happen. We were reminded that God does answer prayers, not in our time, but in his perfect timing.

We got really involved with what the sisters were doing. We went to visit the lepers in the hospital. We met Michelle the leprosy doctor, and he told us that the biggest problem he had with them, was that they had such a long way to come to get to the hospital. Also, once they saw there patches disappearing, they did not come back to finish their treatment, and of course the leprosy soon returned. So when we explained why we had come, he was over the moon; as this would bring great relief to his busy schedule. He told us of a family who lived in a cave, the mother had tuberculosis and the father and children all had leprosy. They were afraid to come down the mountain for treatment so now the bus would be able to carry the treatment to them.

We used to go to visit the nuns a lot and have prayers with them. One day they took us around the local hospital, we couldn't believe what we saw. The patient's relative's slept at the bottom of the beds and they cooked on primus stoves on the wards. The whole place was filthy; it was little wonder that people ever managed to shake off their diseases.

One day Michelle said he would take us to Hannah Lake; it was the local beauty spot. When we arrived we thought we were in another country, the scenery was spectacular. We were surrounded by every fruit you could imagine right there for the taking. On the way back Michelle said he would take us to meet his family, and we would stay for a meal. When they laid the table we discovered it was only for us. We then realised they would not eat because it was their time of Ramadan. It felt quite strange eating when your host couldn't.

Walking through the streets you could smell the sewage, as all the drains were open and ran through the centre, the stench was awful. We would go to the bazaar at night for japatees; this was quite a visual experience. There were five men sat around a hole in the floor, with a gas flame in it. The procedure was that one man would mix the dough, pass it on to the next man, who would separate it, the next man would shape it, and the next would stick it on the side of the hole to bake. Once done, the last man served it up hot. I think most people wouldn't have eaten them, once they had discovered the way in which they were made.

In order to raise money for food we had to sell Peter's bike. This was upsetting as we had carried it the whole of our journey. One day Andy came in and told us he was going to lend someone his passport, he would get us cheap goods. We were angry to say the least, how could he even think of doing such a thing? I think he realised later what a fool he had been. The Lord was supplying our every need; the local people who were Christians gave us food. One night was quite hilarious. There was a knock on the door and there stood a family of five with a big cauldron of curry. The funny thing was they had all come on one motorbike. It was quite a sight to see them all on it.

At the time of the monsoon, the heat became unbearable in the bus, as the temperature rose to 110 degrees. The sister asked if we could move into one of the vacant mission houses while we were there. It was agreed, so we moved a few things into the house, which we had scrubbed, as it was full of sand. All Ruby did was moan and say she wanted to go home. It was a large house with five bedrooms, the first night we thought it would be heaven to sleep in a proper bed. George arranged the mosquito net and we settled down for the night, but when I awoke in the morning I was covered in bites. We thought it was mosquitoes, but when I showed the nuns, they informed us it was bedbugs and we must get rid of the mattress. Once we took it off the bed, we could see hundreds of little red bedbugs running around the floor. We managed to clear them up and move the mattress to the farthest part of the house.

The next day we got another surprise, our first sand storm. We managed to get everything shut up but not before we got a covering of sand everywhere; it took us ages to clean it all up. That afternoon the local gardener came and settled in our garden to pray, we thought he was praying for us, but I found out later he was actually cursing us. So we just ignored him from then on. It was about this time we really started to seek The Lord as to what he wanted us to do. By this time Ruby was getting to be quite a worry, because she would sit up all night, only to find that in the morning she was covered in mosquito bites. We thought it was time to let her go back home, this decision was later to be confirmed by one of the nuns as the right thing to do. So we bought her a plane ticket, two days later we watched her boarding the plane heading for home. Everything had been so traumatic for Ruby; she was just so pleased to be going.

George, Andy and Peter were invited to go to a Christian's house one night, they were a bit reluctant at first, but they went and on their return, they told us how marvellous it had been. They could feel the Holy Spirit moving in that prayer meeting, and once again the hospitality had been wonderful. George went to see the Minister of Protocol about donating the bus to the nuns. He was sent from there to the customs house, which was a five-mile walk; this was very uncomfortable in 110degrees. It was a long drawn out system. George was to find out what it was like to experience prejudice. He was unable to hail a rickshaw because they wouldn't stop. They even shouted in no uncertain terms, to get back where he came from. He wasn't really safe going out on his own but he had to see the Minister, so we all prayed for his safety every day.

During this time George became really ill with Indian dysentery. I called for the nuns to see if they could help, they told me he would need a drip to keep his fluid levels up. I have never prayed so much in my life. After two days George seemed to be getting worse, he had started loosing a lot of weight; I was worried to say the least. Michelle came from the leprosy centre and gave him some more medication. The catholic priest came and prayed for him. He had lost two stones in such a short time. He was also loosing blood from his bowels, it was getting quite serious, I could tell it was the lining breaking down, I prayed and asked God to intervene, it was now we needed George the most. After two more days he started to make some progress. We realised it was nearing the time for us to make plans about what we were going to do. We had enough money to fly back home. The nuns had offered to help us to get to Australia, but we felt because of George's illness. We should go back home.

There was still a lot to sort out, I remember one night we didn't have any food to eat and I remembered what Charlie used to say to Brenda.

"Don't worry, The Lord will provide?"

We set the table in anticipation just like George Muller had done, and Praise His wonderful name; two hours later there was a knock on the door. Upon opening it, there stood two nuns from the Saint Joseph's order. They told us they were led to bring food, because they knew we had prayed for help. It reminded me of the loaves and fishes. When we had finished eating, there was enough left over for the following day.

It was getting near the time to leave, and George had to take the bus to the customs compound where there were so many rules and regulations. Eventually though everything was sorted. Two days later we were at the airport ready to board the plane for London. Michelle and sister Jesusa came to see us off, we got through customs and onto the plane. I was very sad to leave the sisters, but it had to be. They had arranged for us to be met in Karachi by some other nuns, where we would stay overnight and wait for the next plane. While we were there the nuns showed us around the house and gardens, it was wonderful, they had made all their own stained glass windows. Again they were wonderful people, and they looked after us very well, we spent a lot of that night talking about The Lord and what he had done for us.

The next morning it was up and off early to get to the airport, on the way the nun who was driving got the Land Rover stuck in the mud, and couldn't get it out. George suggested she to put it into four wheel drive and after so doing we were soon on our way. She told us she had always wondered what that lever was for. We were very sad to leave them, we could have stayed in Karachi for a while but we knew it wasn't meant to be we had to leave.

The food on the plane was awful it was all curry, and very hot curry at that, we could hardly eat it. It didn't do George much good either following the dysentery. However, we finally landed at Heathrow. We decided to go up to Scotland to Brenda's and then make a decision on what to do from there. We could have gone to George's mums but there were too many of us and we didn't want to burden her. I know she would have coped but it wouldn't have been fair on her. We must have looked a bit of a state; in fact we all looked half dead. How on earth were we going to get to Scotland? We had no money; however, once again The Lord intervened. George happened to put on a pair of jean he hadn't worn since we left England, and inside the small pocket at the top, he found fifteen pounds. We couldn't praise God enough His goodness endures forever.

We got a taxi to Kings Cross station and then boarded a train for Glasgow. It was a long exhausting journey. Brenda met us at the other end and took us to her house. The next day we had to find somewhere to live, the council said they would give us a tenement flat in Twecar, a village not far from Glasgow on the understanding that we didn't have to pay rent but had to move back to Lincolnshire as soon as possible. The Christians in Ayrshire couldn't understand why we had come home. We too, were also a bit puzzled about that one, but we knew God had His hand on it all, and that's what counted.

We moved into the flat, but all we had was what we had come home with, nothing to sit or sleep on, it was cold and there was no fire. George told us he had seen a pit we had passed sometime earlier. He would go out that night to find any coal fallen off the train wagons. When he came back, he was wet through and freezing cold, he had stepped into a ditch full of water. However, at least we had a warm fire that night. We all had to sleep in sleeping bags on the floor, but we decided no matter what, we were going to make it all work.

The next day George said he needed to go look for work, as well as going to the social to claim some benefits. Peter and Andy also said they would go find work. By the end of the day they all had jobs. George went bus driving, Peter went labouring for a builder and Andy went to work in the office at the fire station. Both Andy and George managed to get some benefits, so off we went to the shops to buy food. One of the neighbours gave us a double bed, which enabled George and me to have the bed, whilst the lads shared the mattress. We went out with a grant we had been given and bought enough carpet to cover the whole floor. It was an awesome sight, all different colour stripes going right through the house. George decided to buy some wood and make his own three piece suite.

We went to the local Nazarene church, the pastor helped us to settle into the community, he introduced us to some of the members and we began receiving bits and pieces. A gift from God, that's what we were told, we didn't ask any questions and just accepted gracefully. The Christians in the church were so good to us. We met a lady called Miss Abercrombie, she asked us to go round and meet her Mum. The next day I took the kids, and she invited us into her cottage and introduced us to her Mum. She was 100years old, and was propped up in bed with a large curtain draped in front of the bed to keep the draft out. She also had a woolly hat and some mittens on. The kids just stared in amazement at this lovely old lady. Sharon broke the silence by saying.

"When you get old Mum, I will knit you a woolly hat."

We all laughed. We enjoyed the visit; it was really nice to meet the old lady. On the way home, I started to get breathless, I thought I had indigestion. John was worried, so I must have looked bad, he said.

"Don't you get poorly Mum?"

The children went to school just around the corner, but they didn't like it because the other kids were very prejudiced and bullied them because they were outsiders. It was hard in Scotland; we were all under the care of the hospital, because we were suffering from salmonella, which meant regular tests at the doctors. Andy decided he should go to Brenda's sister in Ayrshire for a few days to get better. I don't think he could manage to "rough it" as well as the rest of us.

One day when all the men had gone to work, I became really ill with pains in my chest and collapsed, the next thing I remember was the siren of the ambulance. I ended up in Stobb Hill hospital in Glasgow; I'd had a heart attack. The doctor told me that I had an enlarged heart and thrombosis. I was told he couldn't do a thing for me other than give me pills to ease the pain. George would keep coming to visit and find me out of my bed; I would be looking after one of the older ladies on the ward. Things were not getting much better but when I got back home, I was really uplifted when George told me that Mum was coming for a while, she would look after me until I was a little stronger. I was somewhat deflated however, when he told me it was my mum, not his, because I knew I would end up looking after her, rather then the other way round.

By this time we had managed to acquire quite a bit of furniture. George had also been able to get a small car. I was continually praying for the strength to be able to look after my family, I was just sleeping all the time. We knew we had to try and get back home, so George rang a Christian businessman, to see if he had a house we could rent. Two days later, he rang us back to say he had found somewhere, but George would have to go down to have a look at it and discuss what to do next. George told him that he would go the following week. We had arranged for him, Pete and John to stay at my sisters for the weekend. He had decided to take the boys so they could see their nana as she was very poorly. On their return,

George told me what had been agreed. Mr D. would buy the house and eventually sell it to us for what he had paid for it. We could live in it rent free, until we could save the deposit. It was then that I realised that God honours His word. When He said, He would pay us back double for our trouble when we willingly surrender all to Him.

We arranged to move back the following week. I was still very ill; it was only a week since I'd had my heart attack. George hired a van, it was decided that he, Sharon, Mum and myself would travel down in the car, whilst Andy, Pete and John would follow in the van. We said our goodbyes to all the friends we had made; they said they wished we didn't have to go but understood it was for the best. It was a long drive, and then the worst thing happened, we broke down. Mum started to panic but George told her not to worry because Andy would be along shortly. Again God intervened once again, because when George got out of the car, lying on the side of the motorway was a length of rope. Yes! You've guessed it, ideal for towing the car. My mum then said (rather sarcastically).

"Yes, that's right; God will see to things; that's why we're stranded here."
We were waiting about twenty minutes before Andy arrived, and we were soon hooked up and on our way again.

10

We arrived in Grimsby quite late at night; we thought this was good because the neighbour's wouldn't be able to see what we had. I was exhausted and when I got inside and saw the house, I was convinced that George must have walked around with his eyes shut. Everywhere was in such a mess; George, undaunted, said everything would be OK. There was a room downstairs at the back of the house and George put our bed in there. Mum turned around and said she would go and leave us to it she didn't want to get in the way. That was Mum, always diplomatic when it came to hard work and having to rough it a bit. George and the rest of the men got everything inside and he told me to go to bed and rest, saying that in the morning he would take the car and get it fixed, deep down, he and I both knew that it had done its last mile. We were all tired and settled down for the night saying that tomorrow would be a brighter day.

The next day I wasn't much help; I still felt dreadful and could hardly move. George began to get things a bit more organised, he then had to go to social services to see about getting some benefits. He also discovered that his instincts regarding the car were right and we had to scrap it. I was in bed a great deal at this time, my heart had worsened and I was put on Warfarin. I began to experience a lot of flash backs about things that had happened years before. I started to get a recurring dream. George told me that he would lie awake and pray for ages because he couldn't sleep, due to the awful noise I was making. Even the children said they could hear me and it was frightening. I asked God to show me what it was that was causing the problem. He told me that I was crying for my mother. I asked Him to deliver me from the dreams, but they still seemed to go on and on. I realised that the only way for me, was to fast and pray. Even though I was so ill, I fasted for two days. Finally, The Lord delivered me, from them with His promise to be always with me. Thank God for His mercies, they endure forever. I was upset because I really believed that He had wanted us to work abroad, and I now realised the truth, He wanted us back in England.

@ One night, George had to go to a works function and although I was invited to go too I just couldn't manage it, so he took Peter with him instead. That night I lay in bed, with Neil and John with me. Neil was not very old, about nine years but he was very spiritual for his age. We started to pray for each other, John read a part of Revelations to me; it was chapter twenty-two, all about the vision of heaven. As Neil and I prayed I had a vision of us being lifted up in the spirit. I saw the gates of Heaven, which were made of pearls and these pearls were shimmering in the light, they were so beautiful. I could hear wonderful music and saw what I believed were the saints, about six in number, in long robes and wearing satin slippers, just like ballet shoes. There was a really rough road full of large stones leading up to the gates. I saw Jesus way up ahead of me. He turned and waved me forward. I was like a small child again in the vision and I was shaking my head saying.

"I can't do it; it is too hard for me."

He continued to beckon me to follow him. Suddenly, it was as though I was being lifted up high by the saint's in the satin slippers; all I could see were their feet and they carried us to the gates. I saw what at first looked like petals falling. Then I realised they were spots of blood, I saw one spot of blood break into thousands of droplets, and they showered us as we gently rested in His peace, being washed in the blood. This peace was so wonderful and reassuring, I knew whatever happened to me; I would be able to go on. That during these times of trouble The Lord would continue to confirm His strength through me. The Lord said to me.

"As thy days are, so shall thy strength be."

I awoke and looked down, Neil was fast asleep; I knew The Lord had visited us. Both John and Neil looked so peaceful.

We found out that our neighbour next door was called Pat she was also a Christian. However, I was so ill over the next few weeks I didn't manage to get out to meet anyone. After what seemed an age, I began to pick up a bit, and we started to go back to Calvary church. It was good to get back into fellowship with Phyllis and the pastor again. We really got settled into the church, going to the prayer meetings and meeting with the members during the week. George even managed to get his old job back and was able to earn some money of our own. Within a year we had raised the deposit needed for the house. We finally had somewhere we could call our own. George started to do a lot of alterations. One day he decided to go up in the loft to have a look around, it was quite funny, we heard a noise; he had only put his foot through the bedroom ceiling hadn't he? He was saying to the kids whilst his leg was dangling through the hole.

"Don't tell your mum."

We eventually got to know the neighbours quite well and they were very friendly, especially Pat who became a good friend. Pat came round one morning and I shared with her what I had been going through, she said she had come to pray for me. When she began to pray I saw Jesus' wounded side, with the blood and water flowing from His wound. Pat told me The Lord showed her I had been battered as a child. She told me, He had showed her the pain I had suffered growing up. After she had prayed with me, I found renewed strength through the Holy Spirit.

We had been home about eight months, and again I became really poorly. George had taken out medical insurance, so I went to see a specialist. He informed me that he thought I had a degenerate spine. He told me the discs wear and this makes them very brittle. An x-ray later confirmed his suspicions. I had other problems as well and I went to see a gynaecologist. He said I needed to have a hysterectomy and he would get me in as soon as possible. With having the medical insurance we thought it would be quick but it dragged on and on. Then one day I went down to the doctors and I could hardly manage to get back home, I thought I was going to die. They took me to the hospital and I thought this would be it I would have the operation. Later, the nurse came and told me she was very sorry, but they were sending me home. She said she couldn't believe it. Peter got really angry and asked.

"Are you sending my mum home to die?"

I had never seen him so upset. His annoyance didn't cut any ice though, and home I went.

George and all the family were so good at that time. They really looked after me. It was only a short time later that I was admitted to a private hospital to have my operation; this was run by nuns and they prayed for me daily, during and after my operation. George came to see me every night, he was going to work during the day, looking after the house and getting the meals ready etc., By now I had lost so much blood I couldn't do anything other than lay there. The nuns told George that during the operation my heart had stopped, they had started it again by using a defibulator. When George asked me later if I remembered anything, I told him I'd had a dream. I was in a lovely place and I just wanted to stay there because it was so peaceful, the gardens and all the surroundings were so wonderful, why couldn't I stay there free from pain?

Suddenly there was like a big bang and all the pain returned to every part of my body. I explained to George how when I had come round properly, the nuns were at the side of my bed praying for me. They brought me a lovely tape with The Lords Prayer on it. When I got home George had decorated the bedroom and he made me really comfortable. Everyone was so good and did everything they could to help. After three weeks I was beginning to feel a little better. I couldn't believe all the changes that were happening in my body, I felt twenty years younger. Never, had I felt this well during the whole of my life. God had really touched me with His wonderful healing hands. He does promise in His word that He will heal us everywhere it hurts.

Later we got really involved with every aspect of the church. We held a service one Sunday and the local radio came and recorded it. It took a lot of rehearsing. I was really tired but God gave me the strength to sing How Great Thou Art. We really did understand how great He is. In the past year He had brought me through a heart attack, a big operation, as well as having to put up with wearing a steel corset to support my spine, called a lumber dorsal.

We were invited to go on holiday to South Wales by some Christian friends. John had recently met a young girl called Karen, and we invited her to go with us. George had to drive down and we stayed for two weeks; it really was a welcome break, even though George worked quite a lot of the time, pulling a barn down for Reg our friend. Reg had been delivered from alcoholism. He had a wonderful testimony, of how God reached him and cleaned him up and put his broken marriage back together. He told us how his wife Stella stuck by him, and the five children. It was around this time that Kay married Shaun, whom she became engaged to just before we left in the bus. They had a lovely wedding, Shaun was a Grimsby Town footballer and they were very suited.

A few months after the service on the radio, there was a big split in the church, The pastor felt that The Lord was leading him in another direction, this is when the devil really got his hooks into the congregation. It was just one extremely awful time. Some were saying he wasn't listening to The Lord, whilst others said he must do what God is telling him. He finally left the church. We believed it was God's will for his life. However, what about the church now?

George agreed to step in and lead the services on Sundays, he arranged for speakers, as and when he could. He admitted later that he could not have done anything like this, in his own strength. However, he kept the church together the best he could. There was a continued undercurrent it was almost tangible; we began to wonder if God ever would be able to get back in again? The split really bowled our kids over. We should have realised that this was the devil's work sifting through us to see how strong our faith was. Unfortunately some of the congregation failed the test, including our own children. We prayed, and The Lord promised that He would draw them back to Himself in His own time. We could not explain to the children, how so many people professing to love God could cause such upset, especially the deacons and elders the so called stalwarts of the church.

Then came another setback, George was made redundant from his job, it was a good job but the company closed down. He got paid some redundancy money, which he paid out on more treatment for me, as the insurance didn't cover it all. Thank The Lord he wasn't long before he got another job. It was a lot less money but it wasn't as far to travel as his last job had been and they also provided transport. He carried on working, besides all the work he was doing at home. Our next-door neighbour Pat said she didn't now how he did it. He was also still managing the organising of the church. He was eventually moved to work in

Scunthorpe, we felt lead to sell the house and move there.

John and Karen decided to marry, so we had a wedding to organise. I made Karen's wedding dress and George gave her away. It was quite funny at the time of the photos, because the photographer asked for the groom's and the bride's dad. George jokingly said he would have to cut himself in half. We were pleased for John they looked so happy together. Pete met a girl called Sarah and they bought themselves a house in Grimsby. He said he was unable to move to Scunthorpe because he couldn't leave his job. He was thinking of buying his own butchery business. He had a good friend in his boss who was nearing retirement and he had agreed to sell Peter the business.

George went hunting around Scunthorpe to find us a suitable property. We viewed a lot of houses and eventually put an offer in on one, on the south side of Scunthorpe. We were so convinced that we were going to have it we moved a lot of building materials into the garage. Then catastrophe! We were gazumped, so it was back to searching all over again. We managed to get a house in Henderson Crescent, it was more then we wanted to pay and we knew it was going to be a hard to pay the mortgage; we still had twelve years to run on the previous one. We knew if we put God first, He would see to our comings and goings, including our finances. We called the house Jacobs Rest, because we both knew, it would only be for a time.

We got settled into the house, Neil and Sharon into a school, and I was feeling much better than I had felt in years. I was still wearing the corset but I was a lot stronger. I had started to trust God for another miracle. I knew it would be in His time, but that I would be able to discard my steel corset; I just kept on praying. There was quite a lot to do in the house, but we knew that little by little we would work our way through it, in God's strength and in His time.

George was doing well in his job, or so we thought. Neil by now had left school and was going out with a girl called Mary. He and Sharon were both working at the same place as George. He had helped to design the cold store and thought that he would eventually be in charge of it, but it wasn't to be. God obviously had other plans for George. During this time I received my awaited miracle form God. I was out of the corset and hallelujah! He even healed my kidneys as well, which the doctor had told me would eventually fail. I had trusted in my maker and not the doctor. His mercy knows no bounds.

Then we had another setback. George found out he had to go into hospital for an operation. Whilst we were discussing it with the surgeon, I asked him if it was a big operation. He said that he didn't do little operations. He explained to us what it entailed. George was to be cut in half and as the surgeon put it have a lot of plumbing work done. There were also growths on his oesophagus he needed to look at to ascertain if they were malignant. This really made us seek The Lord's face. We don't realise our lack until we come to that point where we know there is only one physician, The Lord Jesus Christ.

It was going to be a long time before George would be able to do heavy work again, if at all. The operation went ahead, and I went to stay at the hospital with him in a little side room. He was looking very poorly when he came back into intensive care. They had to give him a transfusion of eight pints of blood. There were tubes and wires everywhere you could hardly see George. When Sharon came to see him she was frightened, he was so pale. I had to wash and toilet him. They gave me a room next to George while he was in the hospital; I think the nurses were grateful I was there; they were so short of staff. He was in the hospital eight weeks. I stayed for the first four weeks and then I had to go home. I hadn't been home in all that time and there were things that needed attending to. Sharon was seventeen years old at the time; she had done very well, keeping things ticking over. George's sister in-law Anne took me to see George for the remaining time he was in. When it was time for him to come home, George's friend from work took me to pick him up. He was very poorly for a long time after the operation.

It took a while after he came home before he could do anything at all. The doctor told me he had to take away several growths, they had been left from of an earlier operation, but there were no malignant ones. It was a worrying time for us both but we trusted in God for a full recovery. Praise His name, He never fails us or forsakes us if we trust Him. George finally got back to work, he found it tiring, but they put him on light duties until he felt strong enough to do his normal job. It was a busy period for us both. Sharon and Neil were both courting, and it wasn't long before Neil was thinking of getting married to Mary, whom he had met at school. Later Sharon got married, but it turned out to be a bad marriage and it didn't last long. However, she had a beautiful daughter out of it, and has since remarried and has a wonderful husband.

Peter and Sarah found out they couldn't have babies so they decided to adopt. It was at this time that many couples were adopting babies from Romania. They decided they would go to see about getting a baby from there. They asked if I would go with them, so George raised enough money to send me too. Finally the day arrived when we would travel down to Heathrow to catch our flight. I was frightened because George and I had never been apart for a long stretch and we had no idea how long it would all take.

When we arrived in Bucharest and we went to the train station to begin our long journey to Iasa, a small town near the Russian border. The platform was awash with people, mainly tramps and poor people who slept on the station. We had to sit on our luggage or they would have taken it, we dare not leave anything unattended; for fear of it being stolen. The journey was awful, the train was filthy and the toilets had raw sewage in them. I think if Sarah could have done, she would have turned around and gone straight back home there and then. I don't know how long the journey took, I lost track of time, that train was a death trap. The soot was coming in through the gaps where the windows should have been. We tried to sleep but couldn't because we were afraid of something happening. An old woman came into our carriage, we were all thirsty and she gave us a drink of water out of a bottle she was carrying. She also gave us a sandwich of sorts, with some sort of meat in it. We didn't know at the time, but it carried a hepatitis germ in it. We were not to find out until after arriving back home.

After about eight hours, we arrived in Iasa and met by a lady called Anda and her cousin; we loaded our bags into their old beaten up Ford. I looked at Sarah who looked more determined than ever to get home as soon as possible. I looked around, and it was as if we had been transported back in time, to around the 1940s. There were lots of bicycles, hardly any cars, and everything was so old, dirty and dismal. Peter was talking to the driver and explained to him we were hungry and thirsty. He made him understand in his broken English, he said.

"Hotel."

We stopped and went inside but it was more of the dark bread, with the meat in them. Sarah and I refused to eat them, they were horrible but we were so hungry. Anda told us it was a long ride to the flat. She said she had arranged for Peter and Sarah to stay in the flat, and mother Joan, that's what I was called, would be across town in another flat. I protested strongly, telling her I would stay with Peter and Sarah in their flat to help with the baby when they got him. Peter agreed and so it was settled.

At last we arrived at a block of flats and we were to be on the third floor, once more everything was so dirty, and there was rubbish everywhere. Anda and her husband slept in a makeshift bed in the kitchen. I slept in the living room on a bed settee and Pete and Sarah were in a bedroom near to me. The bathroom looked as if no one had been in there for months. The next day, after what turned out to be one of the worst nights of my life, we began sorting some things out for the orphanage. We had also brought Anda some coffee and other things they were really grateful for. I also met Addis's mum Sylvia and his dad across the veranda. Addis was our interpreter along with his girlfriend and they lived with their parents. They seemed to take a bit of pride in their appearance as best they could under the circumstances and were really nice. Anda and her husband Olaf were helping Pete and Sarah to get the baby from the orphanage.

The next morning we had to wait until Anda rang the orphanage to see if we could go to see Ben. We got all the baby clothes and nappies and things we had brought from home for the babies. Sarah was so excited; we prayed that any interference from the enemy would be bound before we arrived. George also rang the previous night so I knew he would be praying, also the church back home would be holding us up in prayer too. I will never forget that trip to the orphanage, we went through the town and came to a place which was surrounded by a seven-foot fence; it was a large area with lots of grass and trees; we were greeted by three ladies in white overalls and Peter explained who we were, they then took us inside.

We went down a long dark passage, the stench of urine and excreta was awful the mess was just overpowering. Surely, this is just the way in to get to another part of the building I thought. We passed a glass door, I peered in and the true reality hit me.

There was about thirty children all sat on potties, and they looked as if they had been there forever. It was at this point that, The Lord brought to mind the vision he had given me all those years before when we were in the bus. The vision was about the pile of dead babies with just one still alive.

In the orphanage it was like they were the living dead. Scores of abandoned children left there by their peers to die. We continued on down that long passage to a huge room with lots of cots in it, rows upon rows of them. I just couldn't ever have imagined that anything like this ever existed, let alone be now stood amongst it. These cots were filled with babies and young children up to the age of four, maybe five years old. Some were crying, whilst others just had a vacant stare on their faces. There was nothing inside of them, just like vacant lots. One little girl about two years old just laid there laughing all the time, it was so pitiful; with no one to talk to them. All they had was some white fluid in a bottle; I suppose it was some sort of milk substitute. When the bottles were collected up later, some of them had not been touched, because some of the babies were too small to feed themselves. There were no members of staff available to feed them. We watched as a woman came and quickly swilled them down and put old rags on their bottoms as there were no nappies after they had been dealt with, which took all of three minutes, the cot sides were slammed up, and that was that until the next day.

We were then shown this very pale and frightened child. He had blue eyes and blonde hair. He was cowering at the back of his cot obviously frightened to death of us. We were told this sick baby was Ben. Sarah and Pete looked at each other, took a deep breath and went forward. Sarah had brought a small knitted blue and white rabbit. She handed it to the baby, and he put his hand out to try and get it, Sarah took hold of one of his small hands and put the rabbit in the other one. His face lit up as she did this. Then the woman in charge said.

"That's it for today you can come back tomorrow." Up went the side of the cot. We then saw the doctor who told us, Ben was very weak and poorly, but there was nothing drastically wrong with him.

I think at this point all Peter and Sarah wanted to do was pick Ben up and bring him home that very night. George rang later, I asked him to pray for the judge, the doctor and all the people in charge of the adoption process. We needed a miracle if we were going to pull this off quickly. We had heard that other people coming to adopt, had been spending up to two to three months in Romania and still going home empty handed, and having to come back and start all over again. We hoped that God would intervene and save us all that.

I knew Ben was very poorly, he was blue around his mouth; he was just twelve months old and would die in this place if something didn't get settled quickly. The following day Peter and Sarah had to go and meet Ben's mum, her name was Valetta. They had to travel to a farm outside Iasa to see her. After they returned, they told me how very poor she was. However, after meeting Pete and Sarah, she had agreed to go with them to the courthouse in Bucharest and sign Ben over to them.

The next day after Valetta arrived, they all set off for Bucharest, with Adey as their interpreter. I stayed with Anda until their return. When they did arrive back, they were very disheartened, the courts in Bucharest were closed and they were unable to find out when they were open again. We all sat and prayed that night and then George rang. I explained to him what had happened. He assured me that he would try and found out if he could get any info from his end. The following day he rang back and said.

"Good news, I have managed to get you an appointment to see the judge in Bucharest."

Isn't God good? He even managed a miracle from England. Even to this day, George doesn't know how he managed to get through. God's timing is perfect.

Over the next few days we were allowed to take Ben out of the orphanage, and back to the flat. I will never forget the look on Sarah's face when she lifted him out of the cot and walked out into the sunshine with him. We had taken some new clothes and he had a proper nappy for the first time. We also had some special food to help to build him up for the journey home although, whenever that would be, no one knew.

11

George rang every night, he told us he could sit for up to an hour trying to get through. He assured us that everyone was praying for a miracle to get us home. One day whilst we were in the orphanage a little girl caught Peter's eye, he went over to her looked at Sarah and said.

"Can we manage two?" Sarah said.

"Yes."

When he went to inquire, the staff said.

"No you can't take her she is gypsy girl and not allowed to leave." It broke Peter's heart; he didn't know what to say. Whatever we said to them, they would not change their minds. That night, I asked Anda why they wouldn't allow us to take the little girl as well. She told me that they are underrated citizens and they were not allowed any privileges. We were very upset, but we knew there was no way to help her.

Sarah and I prayed every morning to ask God to bind the devil so he would not hinder us. Peter almost wore himself out, rushing here, there and everywhere to sort things out. There was endless form filling, rules and regulations. We eventually got everything we needed all but a visa to get Ben into England. We really had to put our trust in God now. When we felt it was time to move, we went with our trust intact and nothing more.

The journey back to Bucharest was a long one. First a car ride, and once more that awful stinking train followed by the airport. I felt so ill; I was bringing up a lot of black bile and couldn't eat a thing. Sarah and Pete were the same and Ben had bad dysentery. I guess he had passed it on to us. We said goodbye to our friends who had helped us, and told them we would let them know when we had arrived back home safely. We just sat and thanked God for what He had brought us through. Sarah, Ben and I, were waiting in the airport lounge, whilst Peter went to sort out the flight details. He seemed to have been gone ages; we thought there must be something wrong. Once more we just sat and prayed, hoping God would move things along a bit quicker.

After about an hour, Peter came back and told us we were allowed to go through into the departure lounge. He told us afterwards that the reason he had been so long was, that they had asked him for a thousand pounds, or they would not let us fly. What a terrible time it was, but with God's grace and His intervention we had achieved in three weeks, what usually took six months of going back and forth two or three times, isn't God great.

When we landed at Heathrow airport, we were to face our biggest problem yet. We had decided to bring Ben without a visa. We were held at immigration for two and half hours. George must have wondered if we had been on plane at all. Finally we were given a temporary visa and we were told we had to re-apply every six months until, they decided he could stay. Home at last, well at least in England. We were finally walking through the last gate when I caught sight of George; it was so good to see him again. He had come down to drive us back home. We all got into the car and set off for home all of us completely exhausted we were still passing Ben from one to another, he was still very poorly. We finally arrived at Peter's house,

I asked George to take me home, it was a wrench to leave Ben I had got quite attached to him now, but I knew I had to leave them alone to get to know each other.

It was only a few days later that I had to go into hospital, I had contracted hepatitis, and unbeknown to me, Peter had being admitted to a different hospital at the same time. I learnt later that I had picked it up from the dirty water in Romania. I had turned a bright yellow, even my eyeballs were yellow; it would have seemed quite funny if it hadn't been so serious. When I did finally get over it I was advised not to drink milk or eat certain foods. I was also told never to touch alcohol ever again but that didn't bother me because I hadn't had any for years, since The Lord had cleansed me from everything that was hindering my walk with him.

Everything seemed to be trundling along nicely; all the family were as well as they could be. However, things were not right in our walk with The Lord, everything was hard work, nothing seemed to be happening; we seemed to be in limbo.

There was to be a traumatic time up ahead, George's Brother Pete, suffered an aneurysm. He had to have a brain operation; we thought at one time that he wouldn't get through it. We asked the church to pray for him, and I am sure it was God's intervention that brought him through that operation. Over the next few years we became quite fond of Pete, and he would visit us regularly.

George had another brother John, who had moved to Australia some years before. We told his mum that we would try to trace him; but to no avail. One day Sarah's mum said she helped to trace people for a hobby. We knew he had been in

159

Australia for a few years but had moved on. He had met and married a kiwi girl. So Sarah's mum decided to look in New Zealand. Within just one hour she had found him. He told her he would ring George later that night. When the phone rang later things got quite emotional, neither one of them could speak, so they agreed they would talk again soon, George was over the moon. John assured us he would get a flight over to England as soon as possible and come to see everyone.

We eventually met John at Heathrow Airport; George didn't recognise him at first. Funnily enough it was our Peter that pointed him out and he hadn't even seen him before. He told us later that he looked like George's other brother Peter.

It was a strange visit for John after all those years. Some of the family accepted him, whilst others didn't. I think he was quite overwhelmed by it all. We had arranged for all the family to get together to meet him again, but it was a disaster, the acceptance was not there, apart from that is, our side of the family. John got on with Peter really well. He had only been back in New Zealand two months when he came back again. This was because Peter and his mum were dying. He missed Mum's death but managed to arrive in time to sit with Pete for a few days, before he died. He and George would take it in turns to sit with their brother who finally died on New Years Eve; George and I, together with our son Neil were with him at the time.

John had returned to New Zealand just before the funeral but he came over again later with his wife. He had two daughters both adopted and two grandsons, but unfortunately, none of them came over with them. George and he would talk about their family life and what they had gone through over the years. George mentioned about the first time he had been in church. John told him he had seen him, because he was also in the church. But they hadn't dared to speak about it to the rest of the family. Especially John, he had kept his faith a secret because of the ridicule he would have received from them all. It was a very emotional time for them, but it was also a relief to let some of their feelings out at last.

Since finding John again, we have visited New Zealand and met his wife's family. We discovered to our delight that the majority of them are born again Christians. We keep in touch with them regularly, and know they keep us in their prayers.

We have since sold our house and are going on with The Lord, and waiting for His leading. We continue to lift the children up to God and know His promise is secure, that He will keep them safe until they are ready to come back to Him.

We have joined the local Baptist church, and take part in a house group. I owe my life to Jesus and I know that through all the trials
and tribulations of my life, He has watched my every step. During all the mistakes, He has been there to pick up the pieces and has also been there through all the joys to rejoice with me. I will go on serving Him to the best of my ability until He calls me home to be with Him. Because He tells me in His word, He has given us a spirit
of a sound mind, and renewed a right spirit within me.

A very inspirational story of her overcoming spirit and determination to get through the trials and tribulations of her life thus far, and her ability through faith in God. Really proud to have been a part of her journey, A true overcomer.

George B

We can forgive and thank God everyday for he is good His mercies endure forever Psalm 136 You cannot have a testimony without a test

I thank God he gave me a soul mate, to get through
Our adventures in the Lord together with our family,
Love you George